THE POWER OF PLUS

GIANLUCA RUSSO

THE POWER OF PLUS

INSIDE FASHION'S SIZE-INCLUSIVITY REVOLUTION

CHICAGO
REVIEW
PRESS

Published by Chicago Review Press Incorporated
814 North Franklin Street
Chicago, Illinois 60610
ISBN 978-1-64160-642-4

Library of Congress Control Number: 2022935011

Illustrations: Natalya Balnova
Typesetting: Nord Compo

Printed in the United States of America
5 4 3 2 1

For the women who changed my life,
and the people who saved it.

CONTENTS

INTRODUCTION

FOR AGES WE'VE BEEN CONDITIONED to live our lives aimlessly chasing the concept of self-improvement: If only I were taller, richer, skinnier. If only I were beautiful. If only I were *different*. We learn to hate the bodies that give us life, to cover them up rather than embrace their sheer beauty and unfiltered humanity. We give in to society's unattainable beauty standards, and unconsciously succumb to the pressure to be "thin enough" or die trying. It's time to take back the narrative.

I embarked on my first unsuccessful diet before I was ten. SlimFast entered my life in middle school; I can still remember its chilled, chalky taste and the embarrassment that came with pulling out those bright-red metal tins during lunch. Soon after, Nutrisystem and Jenny Craig became my misguided big sisters. At sixteen a so-called nutritionist would prescribe me a thousand-calorie regimen to follow, consisting of dry toast, orange juice, vegetables, lean meats, and laxatives every night to purge it all out. I'd soon become addicted, and the encouraging and congratulatory remarks I received after losing forty pounds in the span of two months would only fuel my mania. For school and family photos, I mastered the *suck, tuck, and smize*: stomach in, neck out, mouth closed (to avoid cheek widening from smiles), and eyes perked.

I lived to change the very body that kept me alive. I'd purge, I'd lose, and then within a few months, I'd gain. I'd spiral, yo-yo.

I'd wish for skinny and dream of sustenance. And despite it all, I'd always remain fat.

Our dieting patterns are generational, the toxic hand-me-downs we never deserved. From mother to daughter and parent to child, our views are shaped by how the adults around us live to criticize and critique themselves. We become part of a dangerous cycle, one that builds eating disorders, body dysmorphia, and internalized self-hatred. At one point or another, someone must say no. Someone must muster up the courage to shatter decades of intertwined body trauma so that our sons, our daughters, our future leaders can breathe and live without the fear of taking up too much space.

If you've chosen to read this, you are one of those warriors.

Fashion and diet culture are closely intertwined. For centuries, style and luxury remained reserved for the elite, a limited group of affluent, White, thin, conventionally beautiful folk whose bodies could be manipulated into the smallest of samples. Trends were dictated by the thin, and availability of options followed suit. *The Devil Wears Prada* may be a work of fiction, but its candid, terrifying reveal of the industry's thin-first mantra is an undeniable fact I've come to witness time and time again in my years as a journalist.

From fashion weeks to the halls of Condé Nast—the magazine industry's top publishing conglomerate—I've ventured into the tightest of spaces with the sheer hope of breaking ground, of creating new conversations. But dialogue around size inclusivity in fashion is hardly new. It's just always been pushed aside . . . until now.

In my half-decade experience as a journalist, I've spoken with hundreds of advocates about what true inclusivity means. And what I've found within each of their stories is the deepest grit, determination, passion, and love for change like I'd never seen before. Plus-size fashion is about infinitely more than clothing. It is culture, it is healing, and it is transformative. It is *powerful,* beyond one's wildest beliefs. When done right, a perfectly fitting garment can give you the confidence to rewrite your own happy ending, whatever that looks like.

In the summer of 2019 I dove headfirst into this community, reporting on plus-size fashion for outlets like *Teen Vogue, Glamour, InStyle, NYLON,* Refinery29, and more. And within a matter of months, the stories I uncovered were overwhelming in the best way. Then I hit on a realization: what this community deserves more than anything is a place to share their raw and emotional experiences about what it's like to fight for change in an industry indifferent to the plights of real lives.

That is why *The Power of Plus* exists. This book is a love letter to the hundreds of women, men, and astonishing folk who have turned fashion on its back, injecting inclusivity into its core wherever possible. These are their stories, authentic and honest, even when it hurts.

Not everything can be rainbows and celebrations. Beyond the headlines lay real, harmful issues that fester within this community of tightly knit folk. From racism to online bullying to internalized antifatness, there's no shortage of work to be done when it comes to pushing fashion forward. When writing this book, that topic sat front of mind: What picture do I want to paint about the plus-size fashion industry? Do I, like many others, sugarcoat the disappointing moments, or do I tell the unfiltered truth? Do I share with you all what these models and advocates say in the whispers, or only what the covers of fashion bibles will express?

Well, I know change is real. But change is still new. And the only way to push forward is to offer you unfiltered transparency.

Plus-size fashion is not the future. Rather, the future of fashion is inclusive. That means welcoming of all—not of some, not of a few, not of the randomly selected. And that future is finally starting to take form.

This is the story of how we got there, and where we need to go next.

ROUNDTABLE

INSIDE FASHION'S SIZE-INCLUSIVITY REVOLUTION

THIS BOOK IS DRIVEN THROUGH CONVERSATIONS, some joyful, some painful, but all *real*. Intertwined throughout will be round-tables with selected top names from the industry to share their perspectives and observations in a way they're often not given space to do.

Kellie Brown, creator of the blog *And I Get Dressed*, was one of the first plus-size fashion bloggers I ever connected with. Her style, her exuberance, and her work ethic stuck out as game-changing. In many ways she represents the person I one day hope to become.

Perhaps one of the most notable names in the fight for size inclusivity is Iskra Lawrence, a model turned advocate whose work has made widespread noise for its groundbreaking impact. But beyond that, Iskra is a human trying her best to do better, to be better, and to help more.

My favorite part of fashion week each year is internally selecting which model I think will be the next superstar. Yumi Nu is she. As the first plus-size Asian curve model to star in both *Sports Illustrated* and American *Vogue*, she is creating a lane for representation that has never quite existed.

In conversation, these three women are breathtakingly powerful. Together, they represent how far we've come and how important all this work is.

This interview has been edited for clarity and length.

In your eyes, what is the power of community in being able to enact change?

Kellie Brown: Being able to connect with people around the world who love fashion and don't fit into the thin-ideal has been transformative for all of us. We have really built an entire industry that didn't exist with plus-size people now having access to not only clothing but to new opportunities.

Yumi Nu: Nobody wants to feel like they're alone. People want to connect, and people want to belong. And having community in whatever space you are working in or trying to make change in is huge because a lot of times we're afraid to speak up, and we're afraid to share our voice. But the more we can work together to magnify each other, the less scary it is.

Iskra Lawrence: For me, the community aspect means everything. Like you said, Yumi, that feeling of belonging, I didn't have that for a very long time. Not being scared to open up and knowing that I could be different but still fit in is a beautiful thing to feel. So, community in that sense was uplifting, eye opening, and also meant having accountability. The more that you surround yourself with a community that is diverse, the more you will learn, and the more you will grow and learn together. If you're doing it on your own, you can't possibly create as much change. For me, that community aspect means everything.

YN: It's not just one person on a podium by themselves. It's a whole group and movement of people standing together, and it's so much easier to share your voice and say the things that you want to say when you have an amazing group of people behind you.

IL: Community doesn't have to be a hundred people. Community can just be your best friend. It could be a family member. But having some place where you feel at home within a community of like-minded people is going to make you feel supported and going to help you get back on the horse when you're exhausted.

To that point, this community really is how you choose to define it. Everyone's personal community is different, but one of the most important aspects is this topic of perspective. And Yumi, we saw that with your American *Vogue* cover that showcased a wide spectrum of lived experiences. Because by reflecting and representing is how we can truly enact change.

YN: It's such an important point because looking at some of the movements that happened recently—in the midst of Black Lives Matter and Stop Asian Hate—we're never going to be equipped to speak on every possible perspective because we only have our own. Everyone's going to have a very unique voice. Having a diverse community and knowing when to pass the mic is very important.

You've all had such extraordinary career highlights. Yumi, which stand out as the most exciting and impactful?

YN: Being in *Sports Illustrated* was amazing, and the American *Vogue* cover came shortly after that. For me, that was like winning a Grammy. Not only am I on the September issue of American *Vogue*, but it's the most diverse cover, in my opinion, of *Vogue* to ever exist. The fact that I'm a size 16, the biggest size I've ever been, and I didn't have to change a single thing about myself to be on the cover of *Vogue*—I'm still shocked about it. People are starting to actually change their minds in the industry to a point where they're actually making space where they said that they would make space. And then in terms of community, receiving comments from people online saying, "If I had someone who looks like you." Just us existing can sometimes be like a relief to someone who needs to feel seen.

What is your vision for the future of fashion, and what does true inclusivity look like to you?

IL: The future is understanding that I look a certain way, and that's okay. Never apologizing for who you are and knowing that this is also your chance to speak up for other people who might not have the same privileges as you. And when we say "inclusive," I mean it from the people you employ to the people who are in the manufacturing chain to everyone else.

YN: I hope we leave enough room for people in the future to grow. In order for change to happen with inclusivity and everyone to get to a place where all races, sizes, bodies, sexualities, disabilities are included in the media, people need the room and space to learn. I recognize where the high-fashion industry is at, and that itself is a slow-growing process of getting better, but it's happening. We're in the beginning of a lot of these brands making the change. Iskra pushed for no retouching and changed a whole group of people's minds on how to represent their brand, and we're doing that at fashion week now too. We're here to be a representation and a voice and a push for that change to happen and get better.

KB: The fashion industry has to evolve. This ideal of what's elite, what's desirable, what's aspirational has to change as people have changed. We really need to stop the notion that people in larger bodies can't be aspirational. We are so capable, so creative, and doing all the same things that people in smaller bodies are. The future of fashion has to be more inclusive to survive. But as someone who grew up without any of the brands we have now, it's been everything for me.

And to that younger version of yourself, what advice would you give?

KB: I want younger people who exist in a body that is outside of what is presented to them in the media to know that everything belongs to you, and you deserve every good thing. Your creativity, your brilliance, your abilities are not tied to your measurements. The work we do every day is to kick down doors so that the people behind us have it easier in any possible way. It's never perfect, but my advice to them is to keep pushing, keep taking up space, and to be as unafraid as they can. And if you are afraid, keep moving, because none of us are moving without fear or trepidation, but we all keep going.

IL: At the beginning of my career, you were told you have to be a blank canvas. You were told you have to fit into what the brand wanted. And now we are seeing this shift where *we* are the brand. The brands are coming to us because of what we stand for and what we bring to the table. And that holds so much value, and I hope more models realize that power. You can speak up, for yourself and for others. What I hope the future of fashion looks like is an acceptance that we're all imperfect humans, an understanding of what we can do, what's our part, not being intimidated by that, not being afraid of knowing our power, knowing that as a community we can make more change than just an individual, and just not giving up on it.

1

BUILDING THE MOLD

BEFORE STARDOM, before being named in *People*'s 50 Most Beautiful People, before being crowned the world's first plus-size supermodel, Emme Aronson was turned away for being too fat.

Seated in a luxury penthouse, she waited in full hair and makeup for the photographer to arrive, prepared for the long day of shooting ahead. Little did she know he'd leave an impression that would shape her for decades to come. He entered the room, looked directly at Emme and asked, "So where's the model?" She explained that it was her. He looked her up and down, head to toe, and announced, "I'm not going to shoot that fatty," turning on his heel and storming off set. Emme recalls him slamming the door so violently on his way out that picture frames on the walls shook with his rage.

"I was frustrated; I was hurt. I took it personally, but I knew that it was wrong. This is not the way any woman or person should be talked to."

That feeling of being too big, too bold, too boisterous is one that all plus-size folk can relate to. Because in a society formed without our size in mind, squeezing into its narrow lens is beyond harrowing. It is, at times, emotionally debilitating. Those direct attacks on one's size—like in Emme's experience—are the ones that hit deepest, because while many in today's world will restrict their antifatness to judgmental stares and behind-the-back conversations, those who proudly present it outright fearlessly foster hate.

The brazenness in which some hate other human beings for their sheer humanity is perhaps one of the most terrifying situations to face. And Emme is not alone—We can all likely recall the exact moment our size was used to instill humiliation in our minds.

Like the summer before my senior year of college, when a family member confidently told me that I'd never be an on-air journalist because viewers simply would never want to watch anyone who looked like me.

At the time, I was the smallest I'd ever been. But that moment felt like the whole world and its heavy, antiquated ideals were dropped on my chest.

Emme's photographer that day eventually returned to set, demanding that the only way he could photograph her was to "shoot her sexy," ripping apart the fibers on her garments to expose more skin. His reaction mimicked many at the time who thought curvy women could only be used for their sex appeal (thus the influx of nude editorials of the '90s).

Before the days of body acceptance, before curves were celebrated and even coveted, being "too big"—both within and outside the fashion industry—was painted as being the deepest pit of personal failure. Women of the twentieth century were stripped of their voices, taught and told that if their body was the "other," there was simply no place for them to be the glamazons they aspired to become. Fashion, beauty, luxury—all of it was reserved for women of the right size, the right race, and the right social status.

But Emme is living proof of what can happen when you refuse to be silenced.

That day was almost enough to break the new model. Taken aback by the experience, Emme took a sabbatical from the industry, unsure how to proceed. But she received an exciting call only a few months later: she'd been chosen for *People*'s 50 Most Beautiful People special, a momentous stride for any woman, regardless of size. Determined to change the industry from the inside out, she returned, carving a new path with each cover, editorial, and press appearance she booked.

Two years later, she ran into that photographer again. He'd seemingly forgotten their past encounter, instantly recognizing Emme for her recent milestones and expressing his enthusiastic desire to shoot with her. Like the woman of great power she is, Emme responded, "We actually did work together a couple of years ago, and I want to thank you so much. Because of you, I'm in this industry."

Coming from a journalism and real estate background, her transition to modeling was far from conventional. On a lunch break from her real estate job in 1989, Emme stumbled across an article about a small plus-size modeling agency being advertised in an in-flight magazine. Intrigued, she jotted down the address, hopped in a cab, and headed down to the agency's office, where she was signed on the spot. Six months later, Emme left that agency to sign with Ford Models, and the rest is curvy history.

Within just a few years, she went from reporting the news to gracing magazine covers, running her own clothing line, making *People*'s 50 Most Beautiful People list twice, and demanding respect from those who tried to stand in her way.

Emme's fearlessness through strenuous moments is reflective of the women—and community—before and after her who have fought to dismantle this world's horrendous and toxic beauty standards. Because plus-size women have always existed and have—for centuries—been celebrated as beautiful aspects of human life.

The Venus of Willendorf—dated back to over twenty-five thousand years ago—depicts a woman of incredible curves, named after the Roman goddess of love, fertility, and ideal beauty. In the eighth and seventh centuries BCE, the Greeks carved sculptures of women with large hips, breasts, and full stomachs, far different from the bodies we see advertised in mainstream swimsuit campaigns today. During the Renaissance, Titian's *Woman with a Mirror* and Rubens's *Venus at a Mirror* are but two notable paintings from the era of women with such physiques.

From the walls of the Louvre to the covers of *Vogue*, plus-size women are visible in profound ways. So why has the fashion industry tried to convince us otherwise? In our social media–first culture, many mark the start of plus-size fashion as beginning in the late 2000s when curvy girls took the Internet by storm with their stigma-shattering confidence and body activism. But long before we spent hours scrolling through the highlight reels of our favorite supermodels, women fought hard to bring to light a future we can all celebrate within.

Among one of the first was Lena Himmelstein Bryant Malsin, a Lithuanian immigrant who launched what would become the revolutionary brand Lane Bryant. After coming to the United States in 1895, like many immigrants Bryant worked as a seamstress, eventually selling her own lace negligees and silk gowns. And in 1904, in an effort to provide for her son after her first husband's passing, she rented a storefront on Fifth Avenue in Manhattan that would become a leading destination for curvy women.

With the help of Lena's second husband, Albert Malsin, Lane Bryant became a go-to destination for maternity clothing. Upon expansion, the brand saw an enticing hole in the market for extended sizes, and by 1923 its plus-size division had quickly taken over in sales, according to the Jewish Virtual Library. Lane Bryant helped solidify the term *plus size* in many of their original advertisements, first deeming it "Misses-Plus Sizes."

By and large, the industry referred to this division as "stout-wear." Lena's husband, Albert, began to lead the expansion of the brand, surveying over forty-five hundred Lane Bryant customers by analyzing their bust, waist, and hip measurements, according to the *New York Times*. Cross-referencing those numbers with data from life insurance companies, Albert found that different women hold weight in different ways, though this categorization still widely failed to encompass the full spectrum of bodies. As reported by *Women's Wear*, he divided women into three categories:

Type A: Women with a big bust and small hips.
Type B: Women curvy throughout the whole body.
Type C: Women with a flat bust but large stomach and hips.

Albert's research made one point clear—a point many still refuse to accept even a century later: plus size is, in fact, not one standard size but rather a varying spectrum. While the American ready-to-wear industry quickly expanded over the years to come, a national sizing method wouldn't be established until the turn of the century, causing confusion among designers and consumers. The number of plus-size women was growing at an unstoppable rate, but multiple factors prevented them from being seen within the fashion industry: stigmas, access, and economic turmoil. It was evident that dressing for curves would be much different than for the champions of the Gibson girl aesthetic of the early 1900s, and most designers were not up to the task.

A June 1915 issue of *Women's Wear* featured an article entitled "How Many Fat Women in Your Town?" that pointed to the rise of curvy women nationally. As they grew in visibility, however, so did judgment. Multiple *Women's Wear Daily* features referred to stout women as being "freaks." A 1920 editorial was entitled "Even the Freaks Want to Look Nifty."

This fatphobic stigma created boundaries from the beginning, forming a divide between straight- and plus-size fashion before there were even established terms to differentiate the markets. According to research conducted by professor Lauren Downing Peters of Columbia College Chicago, major fashion titles during this period worked alongside the medical industry in fomenting bias against plus-size women. This was aimed particularly at villainizing plus-size Black women. Their bodies became public domains for harassment because of size, race, and femininity.

Much of that can be traced back to the invention of the BMI (body mass index) and the famed and fraudulent "obesity epidemic." Created in the early nineteenth century by Adolphe Quetelet—an academic scholar who specialized in astronomy, mathematics, statistics, and sociology—the BMI was never intended to be a mass measure of health and risk status. Rather, it was a mathematical calculation created to find the size of an "average man" to better understand the spectrum of sizes within the population at large. The creation of the BMI, however, centered on a specific type of body—predominately White European men—while ignoring the vast differentiations across genders and race.

Two hundred years later, the BMI has become the pinnacle of health, despite never being a science-backed measure of such. Rather, it has stigmatized obesity and been used as a weapon to shame and degrade those who fall within its tight bounds of overweight and obese. As BMI obsession grew into a weapon of hate, its reach has penetrated every aspect of life, from workplace discrimination to medical fat shaming and, yes, even to fashion.

Building momentum toward plus-size fashion stalled when the Great Depression hit. The market remained stagnant for years, with department and trade stores slowly instilling change to less media popularity than before. Soon after came the devastation and triumph of World War II, issuing America into a new era.

Over the next years, the National Bureau of Standards began research on the first national size chart: ranging from size 8 to 38, this new chart was based on the measurements of the bust, hip, height, and waist. This remained the norm for many years, and while this sizing guide brought some unity to the design process, it didn't encourage designers to produce a full range with their collections. Many refused to abide by it, creating their own sizing models that progressively got smaller, eventually shifting the tiniest size of an 8 into a 0.

Ultimately, it wasn't until the late 1960s that change picked up again at a pace no one could predict. A major proponent for that: Black women.

The 1960s brought the start of the fat acceptance movement, a charge to end bias and stigma against the plus-size community. At the helm of the social reform movement were Black women who, for centuries, had celebrated their figures. Taking to the streets, they made their voices heard loud and clear, conducting a "fat-in" in Central Park to partake in the burning of diet books. The National Association to Advance Fat Acceptance was then founded in 1969 to aid in improving the quality of life for the fat community. Through the protests that followed, fat women came to form a rebellious, tight-knit group. That community was key: no longer were fat women made to feel outcast. The fat acceptance movement showed them that they were not alone in the long battle ahead toward equality, and those bonds are what helped usher the plus-size fashion industry into a new era.

The 1970s brought the initial waves of change within the modeling industry. With a customer base clearly established by the fat acceptance movement, there was no denying the fact that plus-size women were growing in both number and size, and retailers began to catch on. Many department stores began extending their size ranges, looking for curvy models to photograph for their catalogs.

Vanity sizing became increasingly popular, a new charting method that strongly reflects the one we use today. Gone were the days of size 8 to 38; say hello to 00s and 14s.

In February 1978 a theater aficionado by the name of Mary Duffy was told that Jordan Marsh, a Boston-based department store, was searching for curvy models for their upcoming catalog. She applied and landed the gig, doing as many as twenty-one advertisements for the brand over the course of a month. And Duffy wasn't alone; there was a similar change happening nationally, and it was only a start.

After a year of work in the industry, Duffy formed what would become one of the first plus-size modeling agencies: Big Beauties/Little Women. According to a 1984 United Press International article, the agency represented nearly eighty models within its first five years of conception, ranging from ages seventeen to sixty and sizes 12 to 18. Duffy's agency also represented the petite sector, signing models 5 foot 4 and under. In 1988 she sold her company to Ford Models, which would become a leader in the curve market for many years.

Editor Carole Shaw launched *Big Beautiful Woman* magazine in 1979, the same year Duffy started her agency, signaling a change in the editorial world. The following year brought the launch of Marina Rinaldi, one of the first luxury clothing brands for plus-size women. And just like that, there was a spark that couldn't be put out. Designers like Mary McFadden, Oleg Cassini, Givenchy, Óscar de la Renta, Adrienne Vittadini, Pauline Trigère, Bob Mackie, Nolan Miller, and Liz Claiborne also began producing larger-sized collections.

Over the course of the next decade, change was constant, so much so that a 1991 issue of the *Sun Sentinel* labeled plus-size fashion as being one of the fastest growing industries at the time. The article reported that the market had gone from a worth of $2 billion in 1977 to $10 billion a decade and a half later, an annual growth of between 25 and 35 percent. There were buckets of money to be made, and statistics from the 1980s clearly proved that.

In eighty years' time, plus-size fashion had gone from a miniscule storefront on Fifth Avenue to a mainstream movement that was rapidly expanding. And come the 1990s, there was a new cause for celebration within the industry: the rise of the first curvy supermodels.

"These women that were unknown before became, quote unquote, overnight sensations because they were loud, they were bold, they were body, and they were like, 'Enough is enough. You're not going to shut me down anymore,'" Emme recalls.

Emme wasn't alone: Other women also began to rise the ranks, including Peggy Dillard, Sharon Quinn, Mia Tyler, Catherine Schuller, and Sophie Dahl. They were unstoppable, showing everyday women that they, too, were worthy of feeling as bold as they desired. But that didn't mean change would be easy.

While the 1990s gave curvy models a new level of visibility, it also brought backlash from gatekeepers within the fashion industry who were reluctant to change. From photographers to editors, many wanted the large paychecks that came with editorial shoots, but few wanted fat girls on their film. Stylists would often unleash hell on models, constantly expressing their distaste and embarrassment for bodies that didn't fit sample sizes. It was enough to make some give up, but not Emme. "If I didn't stay in this industry—if I left because of what somebody said to me, made me feel bad, and I took it personally—I would not have [been able to contribute to] the most illustrious, beautiful, emotionally rich, satisfying, and culture shape-shifting movement."

She adds, "Don't let anybody change your path or your direction. Sometimes just look at it as your fuel."

Alongside Emme at the time was Kate Dillon, a former straight-size model who left the industry years prior to focus on eating disorder recovery. She returned in 1995, signing with Wilhelmina as a plus model (like Ford Models and Pat Swift's Plus Models agency, Wilhelmina—first established in 1967—had also joined the movement as a leading representation for curvy girls). And from day one, Kate's intention was crystal clear: to break down barriers within the industry for women of all sizes.

"I went into it like, 'I want to be in *Vogue*. I want to have a makeup campaign. I want to do all the things that cool 'regular' models are doing. But I'm going to do it as a size 10/12 and I'm not going to apologize for it ever again,'" Kate explains.

She'd accomplish all of that in just a few years.

Throughout her career as a plus-size model, Kate contributed greatly in showing that curvy girls could excel in all aspects of the industry. By 2001 she'd appear in a Gucci campaign, *People*'s Most Beautiful People List, a campaign for Isabella Rosselini's Manifesto perfume, a *Vogue Paris* editorial styled by Carine Roitfeld, and eventually, in 2002, a feature in US *Vogue*'s first Shape issue, making Kate the first plus-size model to ever be featured in the legendary fashion bible.

"When we showed up to a job, we felt like we were really a part of it; we felt like we were showing up to a revolution," Kate explains. "Every job mattered; every image that went out there of a full-figured or a curvy girl looking really beautiful and really modern mattered. We knew it."

Kate dealt with her fair share of struggles. Many times, stylists would assume that the sample sizes wouldn't fit her, and so instead of having her try them on, they'd shoot her naked. Some photographers simply wouldn't know how to shoot a plus-size girl, and an awkward and uncomfortable feeling would soon fall across the set. Even when paired with a legendary photographer like Helmut Newton—who shot her first US *Vogue* editorial—Kate could sense when the creative team behind the shoot simply didn't understand her curvy figure.

But for Kate, negative experiences were a rarity. Her outspoken enthusiasm and rebellious attitude toward the industry revealed its strength quickly, showing many fashion icons that she could nail any job at a size 12 just as well as when she was a size 0. Much of her work wasn't pushing for solely plus-size representation but body image and acceptance in general, stressing the spectrum of women's figures and how different each one can look and hold weight. "Nobody even really talked about my body, and that's what my vision was. It wasn't like, 'Oh, she's a plus-size model.' It was, 'That's Kate Dillon. She's a model. And she looks like this.'"

Many of the opportunities for plus-size women in luxury fashion stemmed from *MODE* magazine, a short-lived but impactful publication that launched in 1997 by publishing veterans Julie Lewit-Nirenberg and Nancy Nadler LeWinter. Under the helm of editor in chief Abbie Britton, *MODE* was the first plus-size high-fashion glossy to grace newsstands nationally, featuring models like Emme and Kate on multiple covers.

Model Angellika graced the cover of *MODE* three times, eventually becoming the first curvy model to be inducted into the International Model Hall of Fame in 1999. Angellika originally joined the industry as a straight-size model before later transitioning into the plus sector where, she explains, she found the career to be much more lucrative. While curvy girls were routinely offered less than straight-size models—Emme refers to them as being "second sisters" for this reason—there was far less competition to satisfy the increased demand, thus allowing Angellika and her cohorts to work constantly.

Her experience as a biracial woman in the industry was different in many ways from that of Emme and Kate, and often served as a reminder of the systemic racism that needed to be dismantled both within and outside the plus-size fashion community. One experience, in particular, sticks out in her mind.

"I was doing a shoot for Evan's department store out of London," Angellika explains. "And we went to this owner's restaurant and everything was cool. But then he saw us on the street, and he did not utter a word to me. And that was a wake-up call. I was like, 'Oh my God, that's full-on racism.' He didn't want people to know that he knew me."

Racism within the fashion industry has prevented many models of color from gaining the same exposure as their White counterparts, despite talent. It's an obstacle Angellika battled from time to time, but one she used to encourage her to push harder. Like one instance when *MODE* was set to put a popular White model on its cover yet again. Confused as to why she wasn't considered, Angellika paid for her own airfare and lodging out to L.A. to be a part of the shoot, eventually ending up on billboards in an infamous slip dress that then became one of the most popular campaigns in the magazine's run.

Another popular cover: Queen Latifah, a hard get for *MODE*, but one that put them on the map as a major fashion trendsetter. "Having her represent women in a powerful way [was transformative]," says Corynne Corbett, former executive editor of *MODE* who later became the editor in chief in 2000. "I worked so hard to get Queen Latifah for the cover, and it was a moment where people really recognized *MODE* for what it was."

In addition to launching the careers of many models, *MODE* gave designers the opportunity to have their plus-size clothing featured in a rising high-fashion publication, allowing them to experiment with extending sizing if they hadn't before. Richard Metzger became a regularly featured designer in the magazine, as did Marina Rinaldi. *MODE* was not only a launching pad but also a revolution of what the future of fashion could look like. The 1990s were only the start, and if that decade had shown anything, it's that women were ready for a curvy revolt.

But disaster brought all momentum to a halt.

The terrorist attacks of 9/11 led to *MODE* closing down shop; just months prior it was in talks of being sold. With the publication gone from newsstands, designers no longer had a perfect platform to showcase their plus-size lines, unable to inform the average American woman—who, at this time, wore a size 12/14—of their extended sizes. Many plus-specific brands were forced to shutter while others returned to straight sizes only.

Other issues arose. For an array of reasons—like financial stability, accessibility, and the desire to lose weight before giving in to a higher price point—plus-size women weren't spending their money on luxury clothing. Without *MODE*, curvy models were far less represented in major campaigns and editorials, and visibility decreased drastically.

The plus-size fashion industry was back in a rut. Despite monumental progress since the fat acceptance movement, all remained at a standstill as the industry entered a new post-9/11 era. It would take something groundbreaking to revitalize plus-size fashion, and no one quite knew exactly what that was.

The answer, however, was right at their fingertips: the Internet.

2

THE DIGITAL TOUCH

F EW MODELS warrant a first-name-only reputation. Toccara is among them.

In 2004 Dayton, Ohio, native Toccara Jones made history as the first plus-size contestant to compete on cycle three of *America's Next Top Model*. Her exuberant personality—who could forget when she entered the audition room and proudly declared "I'm big, Black, beautiful, and loving it" to the judges panel?—quickly landed her fan favorite status. And her experience on the show would live on for years to come, serving as a catalyst for the next generation of curvy models.

Three years post-9/11 and the end of *MODE*, the plus-size fashion industry was at a standstill. Yes, curvy girls were still working, shooting campaigns for retailers globally, but the remarkable pace of progress had slowed to a crawl, along with most mainstream representation. Toccara revitalized it all.

The twenty-two-year-old's intentions for competing were clear: Toccara was going to be the world's first plus-size, Black supermodel, whether the judges—particularly Janice Dickenson, whose pointed words aimed to hurt the young hopeful—recognized it or not. Week after week, not only did Toccara deliver stellar photos but she also constantly reminded viewers that her size and identification within her Blackness were not burdens to shed. Rather, they made her remarkable and gave her the power to live in her own skin.

"I remember watching and wondering why she was treated differently just because she's a bigger size, and even though they may not say it's because she's a Black woman, we know in the back of our heads that had a huge effect," says Jazzmine Carthon, one of two model winners on season 16 of *Project Runway*.

Jazzmine watched cycle 3 of *America's Next Top Model* live from her home in Compton, California, when she was just a child. She credits Toccara for sparking her desire to model, opening her eyes to the then-miniscule world of plus-size fashion. Jazzmine comes from a family of proud plus-size women, yet still found herself trapped in a generational curse of crash diets. Like many, she found it difficult to break the cycle and live unapologetically in a body that didn't need to be changed. But through her teenage years, freshly inspired by Toccara's greatness, Jazzmine let go of what society told her was beautiful and redefined the standards on her own terms. She went on to audition for *ANTM* twice, eventually landing *Project Runway* upon moving to New York City. And in a similar way that Toccara touched her, Jazzmine hopes her story helps inspire the next generation of Black, curvy girls.

"Back then, every woman I knew with curves was trying to fit into this tiny little box that we literally didn't fit in," Jazzmine recalls. "And here comes Toccara: huge breasts, hips, really thick thighs, my skin tone—it was the representation that I didn't know that I needed at the time."

Essie Golden, creator of #GoldenConfidence, recalls, "Even the scene in one episode of Toccara rolling over and eating the rotisserie chicken in bed was iconic. She was unapologetically herself, and I think to see a woman of her size do that and be absolutely stunning and breathtaking was remarkable."

Like Jazzmine, Essie was inspired by Toccara to give modeling a try early on in her career, prompting her move to New York City after cycle 3 went off the air. Success didn't come as instantly as she'd hoped, but that didn't stop Essie from following the signposts Toccara had left along the way on how to be a proud Black girl in a skinny, White world.

"She showed up on set, 100 percent herself, ready to go and serve better than anybody else, in my personal opinion, on that show," Essie adds. "She felt like someone that you want to get drinks and have a girl's night out with, and the fact that she doesn't have the career or get the recognition that she deserves is truly hurtful. Anytime I do any type of interview, I always make sure that I mention how Toccara changed the game for me personally, because that's the honor she deserves."

The goal of representation has become skewed over the years, often minimized into a quota to satisfy viewers. But as made evident by Toccara and the countless women she influenced, true unprecedented representation has the power to alter and save lives.

Representation matters for a reason. Toccara's legacy is living proof of that.

Despite serving on set week after week, Toccara's time on the show was cut short in what many—including Jazzmine and Essie—believe was an unfair elimination. In her final photoshoot on *ANTM*, she experienced an all-too-common difficulty for plus-size models: the clothes just wouldn't fit.

The show's stylist got heated with Toccara, blaming her for being too curvy to squeeze into the clothes she'd pulled. Despite having her measurements and dressing her week after week, some-how, that one episode, nothing seemed to fit, almost as if an excuse was needed to rationalize her elimination. The awkward scene served as a reminder: Toccara was bold, powerful, and confident, but she was still a plus-size woman living in a thin-first world, no matter how much she laughed it off.

Essie can now relate to that painful experience. She's shown up countless times on set "ready to serve a look," only to have not one of the options pulled fit her. In one instance, she sat down in the hair and makeup chair, just to hear the White stylist exclaim, "What do you want me to do with this?" Fatphobia, racism, and colorism directly go hand in hand.

Through the eyes of Jazzmine, Toccara had two strikes against her: Yes, she was plus size. But she was also a dark-skinned Black woman, both of which made her a "hard sell" to viewers, Jazzmine believes, based on her own experience in the industry where, when she began modeling, she was labeled as the "nonthreatening Black girl next door." While Black women constantly break down barriers in the size-inclusive fashion space, as Toccara did, society's refusal to view them as "palatable" erases their stories from the narrative. "If you have a closer proximity to Whiteness, you have a better image to promote in the mainstream media and you have a better chance of being successful," Jazzmine adds.

A few years post-*ANTM*, Toccara was featured in a multipage spread in *Vogue Italia*'s all-Black 2008 issue, photographed by the legendary Steven Meisel. It was a moment that should have launched Toccara into supermodel status. But it didn't, because—according to many interviewed—she was simply too curvy, too confident, too Black.

Toccara's start coincided with the rise of social media, LiveJournal and Tumblr becoming among the most popular platforms. In this newfound space, plus-size women finally had somewhere to go to address their concerns and speak on how being fat had directly affected them personally, both the good and the bad. For the first time, plus-size was not the "other." It was the common thread that began to pull together an online community of future advocates.

Circa 2008 a wave of plus-size women began to expand the online discourse around fat acceptance into fashion, launching blogs that, while rooted in size-inclusivity, were simply entertaining pastimes to showcase their personal style. Among them was Marie Denee, a business-minded fashion mogul with the dream of opening her own plus-size boutique, aimed at creating a space she wished she'd had growing up.

"Everything was uncharted territory," Marie recalls.

The rise of plus-size fashion as we know it is directly correlated to the rise of social media. Not only did it give women an outlet to express their personal styles and life journeys but it also gave them direct communication with brands that, like these women, were new to the online scene. The original plus-size fashion bloggers, including Marie, were able to redefine what the plus-size customer looked like from a fashion perspective, igniting a flame in many brands to widen their size ranges and start paying attention to this newly vocal but long-awaited woman.

Determined to share resources for curvy girls, Marie launched *The Curvy Fashionista*, a blog that would become a go-to destination for size-inclusive media coverage. Seeing the instant reaction to *TCF*, Marie quickly learned that what she was creating was more than a resource: it was part of a movement.

That all clicked for Marie five years into the creation of *TCF* when Marina Rinaldi brought a handful of leading plus-size bloggers to Milan to shoot their Women Are Back campaign. It was a life-changing experience she'll never forget. Marie and eleven other bloggers in Italy, flaunting their curves and getting paid to do it.

In 2009 Marie would expand *TCF*'s reach to work with an exciting, never-before-seen kind of event: the very first Full Figured Fashion Week.

Created by former party promoter and sometimes-model Gwen Devoe, Full Figured Fashion Week was everything that

New York Fashion Week wasn't: inclusive, riveting, and full of opportunity for up-and-comers.

"The most important thing for me in producing Full Figured Fashion Week was to make sure that it was on par with what I had seen under the tents at Lincoln Center," Gwen tells me. "I wanted the most beautiful models, I wanted a variety of different sizes, I wanted all nationalities."

With Ashley Stewart as the brand's first corporate sponsor, Gwen was off to the races. Everything—from the set design to models to gift bags for attendees—had to be just perfect. And come day one of Full Figured Fashion Week, it was. Until Gwen's pager began to go off.

On the first day of Full Figured Fashion Week 2009, news broke that music icon Michael Jackson had passed away. All but one of the few editors who'd promised to cover the event instantly backed out. "It was a pivotal moment because we worked so hard, and now no one was going to know about it. But that is why I always pay homage to the plus-size fashion bloggers in attendance. They wrote their stories, they posted, they took pictures, they [brought it alive]."

She adds, "For the first time, we all came together in sisterhood, we supported each other, and we looked fabulous doing it."

Gwen recalls the first Full Figured Fashion Week—which, despite its name, initially was only a weekend long, filled with both runway shows and business workshops—as being "strangely liberating," filled with tear-jerking moments of supreme bliss and shock at what she'd pulled together.

Year after year, Full Figured Fashion Week grew in popularity and reach. It was the go-to destination to meet fellow fat fashionistas, networking and connecting directly with those whom you admired so deeply online. And even when the budget fell short, Gwen was devoted to making the event bigger and better than years prior to show the industry that this community was not a fad, not a passing trend. "We live this life every single day, trying to find clothes, and we love fashion. We spend so much damn money!"

What Gwen could never predict, however, is the doors that Full Figured Fashion Week would open, not only for brands and designers looking to expand into the plus-size space but also for new hopefuls to create unique careers of their own. Like Gabi Gregg and Nicolette Mason, a power duo who would eventually go on to partner on their own plus-size fashion brand, Premme, that would leave its mark on the industry despite a short-lived run. Before the two were best friends designing chic, timeless pieces, they each carved unique roles for themselves in the creation of the industry: Gabi as an influencer and model and Nicolette as a magazine writer.

Originally from California, much of Nicolette's style growing up developed from her mother's Iranian heritage. Culture, she explains, played a huge role in her upbringing as she navigated life at the intersections of being plus size, queer, Jewish, and Middle Eastern in L.A. After high school, she jumped coasts, opting to study design and management at Parsons School of Design in New York City.

Plowing through internship after internship, Nicolette struggled to envision her own space within the fashion industry, somewhere her unique voice could not only be heard but also celebrated. Upon graduation, she began working at an architecture, interiors, and branding firm, balancing her new nine-to-five with her side hustle: a little (unpaid, at the time) blog, serving as her go-to creative outlet. "Our blogs weren't about ourselves. They weren't about competition. It was really about creating pathways for people to feel beautiful and to have a place in fashion."

Little did she know that a turning point was right around the corner.

After picking up steam online, Nicolette was asked in 2009—alongside Gabi and fellow blogger Sakina Benachich—to write for *Vogue Italia*'s curvy vertical, a newly founded destination for plus-size women. As Nicolette puts it, "It felt like a really fucking big deal."

"I knew the conversation online was not just happening online anymore," she says. "It was starting to take hold and take foot in real-world settings. We were seeing that in magazines—again, from a very, very small extent—but coming from zero, it was something. We were starting to see it in editorials, we were starting to see it in what kinds of headlines were being made when plus-size models were cast in campaigns. And of course, the more pressure there was online, by consumers and by body positive bloggers and fat activists, slowly we started seeing more demand for retailers to catch up to the conversation too."

Magazine articles like "More Overweight Kids Wearing Adult Sizes" became drowned out by headlines like "Fashion First, Whatever the Size," "Will 2010 Be the 'Year of Plus'?," and "Advertisers Embrace a Plus-Size Reality" taking center stage in publications like the *New York Times*, ABC News, and CNN. Intrigue buzzed around who these women were and how, in a society that had told them to hide and self-deprecate, they had acquired so much confidence.

According to Gabi, the answer was simple: sisterhood.

While in college, Gabi stumbled across digital communities specifically dedicated to plus-size women on LiveJournal, a then revolutionary diary-like social networking service. One group that caught her eye was *Fatshionista*, "And they really introduced the concept of fat politics into my life, and it completely changed my worldview," Gabi says.

She describes that moment as prophetic, her first realization that somewhere, in these hidden corners of the Internet, there were other women existing without the pursuit of weight loss center to their lives.

As the conversation geared further and further politically, young Gabi saw an opportunity to create space for a style-centered dialogue. Taking inspiration from other blogs popping up in 2007, Gabi launched her own a year later—titled *Young, Fat and Fabulous*—motivated, in part, by the lack of job options available because of the recession. What better résumé booster than a digital portfolio that perfectly captured who she was and what she stood for?

It was an instant hit.

"It was spreading by word of mouth really fast," she recalls. "It just goes to show how few resources there were at the time. It all felt very weird and surreal."

With *Young, Fat and Fabulous*, Gabi tackled it all: trends that had previously been "reserved" for thin bodies; where to find stylish options that actually fit and hug your curves; and how to, as she puts it, "make it work," inspired by the iconic catchphrase of legendary *Project Runway* host Tim Gunn. "I talked about, as a plus size woman, how we can make things work for us that weren't meant to fit us." Within six months Gabi had become the It girl. Featured on *Good Morning America* and quoted in the *New York Times*, she was professionally thriving. And on the personal side, it all felt like the ultimate self-healing journey.

"It was the first time I recognized that I didn't have to hate my body and I didn't have to cover up my body. . . . My blog was marrying this concept of dressing to express yourself and introducing that concept to a wider audience where we had only been told for so long that getting dressed was about looking smaller, what to avoid, what not to wear. My kind of mantra was all about dressing for self-expression. We had never had the freedom as fat people to do that before, because it was always about dressing to look skinnier."

Nicolette and Gabi first connected through that popular Live-Journal group. Not only were both women around the same age, but Nicolette's posts about "Chanel shoes and designer bags" caught Gabi's wandering eye. "I was so removed from the world of high fashion, I had never seen someone my size wearing Chanel before or Alexander Wang," Gabi recalls. "She was wearing all these designer brands and accessories that I thought were so beautiful. And so that blew my mind, which is funny to say because now, it isn't like a big deal at all. But then it was like, 'Oh, my God, a fat girl wearing Chanel? What the hell! I didn't know that was possible.'"

For many—including Nicolette, who credits Gabi with pushing her to post more style on her personal blog—Gabi is the ultimate pioneer of the digital plus community, the OG fat girl. In 2010, two years after starting her blog, Gabi created one of the first plus-size fashion meetups titled the YFF (Young, Fat, Fabulous) Blogger Conference. The idea stemmed from that feeling of being othered after seeing a group of straight-size bloggers putting on an in-person conference without including any plus voices. And so, pulling together ten bloggers from around the world, the first YFF Con gave readers the opportunity to connect with these newly famous Internet celebrities, bringing this digital-first community to life in a powerful way.

"We felt like we were on the precipice of something historic," says Hayley Hughes, one of the bloggers featured at the first YFF Con. Based in Melbourne, Australia, Hayley grew up largely ashamed of her body. "If you look at my early posts on my blog, I never shared my legs, and I was really embarrassed to share my arms." Launching her fashion blog in 2006 gave her confidence with each woman she connected with, including Gabi. "Because of blogging, I could suddenly wear a bikini at the beach. And that just would not have been my life without these other women giving me that confidence."

She remembers YFF Con as being one of the most joyous moments in her career, a clear sign of what the inclusive future of fashion would eventually look like. Crammed into a Brooklyn shop, YFF Con showed the unity behind the plus-size community, proving that the message here was so much deeper than clothing or money: It was about the transformative power that comes with being represented for the first time, and how it feels to come into your own body, looking fabulous while doing so.

Alissa S. Wilson, founder of StylishCurves.com, felt similarly, having attended YFF Con as a baby blogger with a knack for fashion journalism. She credits the event as sparking a larger conversation within the online community, proving that plus-size women were ready to show up and give their support, even if it meant traveling all the way to Brooklyn to do so. YFF Con inspired Alissa to eventually start her own plus-size fashion popup event.

At the time, Alissa was also regularly attending New York Fashion Week, one of the very few plus-size journalists to do so. Acceptance there wasn't as common as it was online, and she dealt with her fair share of fatphobic street style photographers and catty PR girls running around Lincoln Center. A part of both worlds, Alissa used that knowledge to connect with brands and designers directly, sitting down to explain to them what exactly the power of plus-size fashion is.

The true power, however, lies in that supreme feeling of connection. Little did Gabi and Nicolette know that some handful of years later—in July of 2017—those community-driven bonds would inspire them to launch their own brand, Premme, that would turn the industry on its head.

Premme was the duo's love child, a beautiful byproduct of their vast work and experience in the space. Everything that brands refused to give plus-size women, everything they were told they could never wear—that fire is what fueled Premme's eruption onto the world stage.

Announcing Premme just one day before its public launch, Gabi and Nicolette could finally share their hidden double lives with the world. They were about to add "fashion designer" to their long list of accomplishments. But not even they could predict what would come.

Within twenty-four hours Premme's entire first collection had sold out.

"Our partners had never seen anything like it," Nicolette recalls. "Our partners were veterans in e-commerce, they were very well seasoned in how online retail works, and they had still never experienced that kind of volume and demand for product."

That moment was proof positive that plus sells.

"The biggest takeaway for us was proving that all of the things these huge corporations with endless amounts of capital and resources were telling us couldn't be done—they have no excuse for at this point. Because if we could do it, if we could do it on bootstraps, it could definitely be done."

Gabi adds, "What differentiated us as designers was that we came from the community. Coming from that perspective, knowing what's missing, knowing the frustration of being a consumer in this space is really what set us apart. . . . How we decided to market our clothing, what models we hired, making sure we had diverse models on both sides, making sure that we went up to a size 30—all of those decisions were made because we come from this community."

Questions like "What's not available to us?" and "Why isn't this already available in the plus-size space?" nourished their design process. Because Premme was more than just another brand tackling an underserved market in pursuit of money or success. Premme was the answer to everything we in the plus-size community could have dreamed of: Premme was the blueprint.

"At the end of the day, including a diversity of body types, ethnicities, abilities, etc., it's not just good business," Nicolette says. "It's just good to do. And people deserve to see themselves in the world, and they deserve to feel included in the world."

She continues, "We thought, 'Why don't we just do this ourselves and prove that it's possible and that all these things that people are telling us can't be done—whether it's using bigger models for e-commerce, whether it's having a larger size range, using bold colors, and making body-con dresses and having cutouts and really centering true body positivity in that conversation—is possible. And it's not just possible, it's not just doable. But it's possible to do it and succeed as a business.'"

The journey to Premme was not easy, however: Gabi and Nicolette struggled to find a brand partner at first, eventually deciding to build Premme on their own with one other full-time employee. Even then, despite widespread acclaim, securing funding to scale the business was a hurdle. How were they to convince privileged men who never had to think much about the space their bodies take up in the world that plus-size women wanted to feel sexy and beautiful in ways the industry had never allowed them? How could they prove the power of community without a shining tech-angle to appease investors' finance-driven minds? How far could they push the boundaries without support from the other side?

Two years later, owing to financial constraints and limitations, the duo decided to close the brand. Despite that, they continue to view Premme as a success as in its short incarnation, they were able to prove precisely what this customer wants and how brands could succeed in this space. Almost a decade since the first YFF Con, Gabi and Nicolette had come full circle: everything they dreamed of—of fighting for plus-size women, of giving them the fashion they truly deserve, of creating space for them to exist in all of their fabulousness—had come true. All because they centered the power of community.

The first time I experienced this power in person was at my first CurvyCon, an annual plus-size fashion conference created in 2014 by CeCe Olisa and Chastity Garner-Valentine. After starting out as bloggers themselves—CeCe recalls pining for a ticket to YFF Con back in the day—the two created the CurvyCon as a way to unite this community and show brands—and the fashion industry at large—that we were here to stay.

I was sent to cover CurvyCon by Fashionista.com. It was only my third season at fashion week, and my first covering it for numerous outlets. Dressed in a salmon suit with a camouflage tote and classic white sneakers, I entered the convention center with no idea how the day would go. Instantly, I was met with love.

From bloggers I'd never met in person to models I'd only interviewed over the phone, each step of the way, I was overwhelmed by the love and inclusivity that possessed that room. Women and men of all shapes, races, ethnicities, heights, and styles filled the CurvyCon, bringing it to life with their passion, loud laughs, and joyous attitudes. It was instantly made clear to me that the Curvy-Con was more than just a stop-and-shop for discounted plus-size fashion. It was a revolution, in and of itself. In that moment, size had brought us all together, but size couldn't be less important. For three days we could all breathe without the fear of taking up too much space.

That feeling of unity is what changed the course of my career, and what moved me to reevaluate my own voice within this community. The surreal juxtaposition between the CurvyCon and New York Fashion Week—which take place at the same time each September—couldn't have been more clear to my then twenty-year-old self. Uptown at the CurvyCon, inclusivity was the norm.

It was a celebration, not just of who we were, but of what we stood for. And downtown at Spring Studios, we were the token—a rare occurrence on the runways or in the seats of major fashion shows.

It was evident in which part of town we were wanted, and on that September morning, I couldn't have cared less.

YFF Con, Full Figured Fashion Week, and similar events showed the industry that after years of building their digital voice, plus-size women were ready to create tangible change. And it was through that first wave of plus-size bloggers that representation began to boom, a feat last experienced in the 1990s. With the launch of Instagram, there was no slowing the pace: Plus-size fashion blogs were a hit, and the women behind them became the advocates and models who would change the world over the next ten years.

Because as the digital space grew, so did the runways, welcoming in the second generation of curvy supermodels who would bring plus-size fashion to the mainstream.

3

THE NEW SUPERS

MODELS AWAIT ONE OF TWO PHONE calls when put on hold for a job. The first being, "You've been released," meaning you've been passed over. The more exciting call, "You've been confirmed," can be life altering.

When Candice Huffine picked up her phone one early 2011 day, waiting to see whether she'd booked one of the most prestigious jobs in high fashion—the annual *Pirelli Calendar*—all she heard from her agent was "You've been—"

In antici . . . pation, the line dropped.

Candice began modeling at fifteen, segmented into the plus market for her size 6 frame. Throughout her adolescence, the young fashion hopeful had never categorized her body as different. But by signing on the dotted line, for the first time in her life, she felt othered for a body that, up until then, had always felt like the norm.

"It was shocking to be knocked back on my heels by a stranger who, for the first time in my life, was telling me that something's wrong with my body when in reality, I was an athlete. I felt great. I was super confident at school. I was happy. I felt cute. I felt obviously very confident because I marched myself to New York City to get a modeling contract that I thought was mine. It was really so sassy," Candice recalls with a laugh, thinking back to that youthful bravery she showcased in those early moments.

If that day had never come, however, fifteen-year-old Candice could have lived in "perfect oblivion," as she puts it. But as social media often does to young girls today, that first casting agent's up-front remarks began to break through her youthful innocence.

Candice began working quickly, appearing in *Seventeen* magazine a handful of times, and working extensively for German and English fashion catalogs (a typical gig for curvy girls of the early 2000s). Flip-flopped from the state of size-inclusivity two decades later, America had yet to truly understand who the curvy customer was, though Europe was on board.

"Curvy women were misrepresented and misunderstood," Candice recalls. "Nobody really knew who she was, what she needed or what she wanted to shop for. I like to say that both of us grew up together: myself in the industry, and then the industry itself. We were navigating this world at the same exact time, growing and figuring it all out."

No matter the label, Candice's determination and pure authenticity—losing weight or changing her shape for a gig or agency was "always out of the question for me"—in those early years is what set her apart from the next era of supermodels, signaling the start of a highly inspirational career (a career that, yes, would include being featured in the *Pirelli Calendar*).

All of that seemingly came into fruition in 2010 when, in an industry-altering move, she appeared alongside three other curvy women for a milestone issue of *Vogue Italia*.

Before social media, magazine covers served as a surefire route to mega success. From *Elle* to *Harper's Bazaar* to *Vogue* and every page in between, landing a major cover not only solidified your spot as a top model but also guaranteed a lucrative and exciting career to come.

Even further, landing the cover of *Vogue Italia* had the power to turn a classic catalog gal into a global sensation.

"We were not proficient artistic models," Candice explains. "We sold jeans and T-shirts for a decade. So getting the casting for *Vogue Italia*—your heart drops to your feet and back up again."

Casting for *Vogue Italia* was far different than anything Candice had ever experienced. Till then, she and fellow curvy girls would show up to set dolled to the max: hair done, makeup perfected, as full glam as they could achieve. Because in an industry where plus was still viewed as the lesser, they wanted to leave no room for interpretation for narrow-minded photographers. Rather than allow them to struggle in figuring out how best to shoot bigger bodies, Candice and her close confidants made it their mission to serve their best angles as soon as they walked through the door. Even if it failed to reflect their personal style, curvy models were trained to be glamazons in ways their thin counterparts never had to.

But *Vogue Italia* was different. This was the big leagues, the Garden of Eden of the modeling world that only few were granted access to. And so, rather than arrive done up, Candice was instructed to come as a blank canvas: "Put your hair in a ponytail, do *not* wear makeup," her agent told her at the time.

"I remember begging him, 'Can I just please wear mascara?' And he was like, 'One swipe of mascara, that's it!'"

Days later, preparing for a planned (and soon to be canceled) trip to Aruba, Candice got the call: "She got the job, honey!" she tells me with a laugh. "If you want something major to happen in your life, book a trip. It was so funny because that was the first time that my husband really realized the nature of this job: things change in an instant, and everything is paused for the dream."

In a room full of designer dresses, diamonds, and sheer fabulousness, Candice gathered alongside fellow cover girls Tara Lynn and Robyn Lawley (as well as Marquita Pring, who appeared within the issue's inside spread) as they prepared to be shot by Steven Meisel. What could have been a terrifying adventure turned into a monumental moment, for the four women and the millions whom they would have an impact on. Together they stood, powerful, united, and revolutionary in their mere presence on set. "I felt so bonded to them. We shared this insane moment in time together," Candice recalls.

Like Candice, Tara, Robyn, and Marquita had been blazing their own trails before their *Vogue Italia* turning point. And in the years to come that would only intensify: Marquita went on to become a fashion week superstar, appearing in runway after runway, campaign after campaign. Tara became an internationally acclaimed cover girl and game changer, and Robyn an outspoken advocate for change across the aisle, on topics from size diversity to health.

That now famous *Vogue Italia* cover solidified the curvy woman's place in high fashion, crushing the mystery around whether she could command space in this sought-after subset of the industry that until then was marked Do Not Enter. Gone were the days of hiding, the days of waiting for her body to change. She was here, and she was more than ready to serve.

"To my five-year-old self, I would say, 'Thank you for knowing your purpose,'" Candice tells me. "Thank you for being a fly-by-the-seat-of-the-pants badass who was like, 'I'm marching up to the steps of this agency in my sneakers and T-shirt to get my modeling contract and make my dreams come true.' There wasn't any overthinking involved: She was so confident; she didn't waver; she knew what she wanted. I remind myself to be that girl again, because the way that she set me up for the future was perfect."

Few things reign as monumental as that *Vogue Italia* cover. It altered the course of the industry, opening new doors and opportunities for women who were more than ready to step into the spotlight and represent those at home who so desperately sought the feeling of normalcy, of knowing their bodies were not the "other" but rather the "common."

Top models of today often refer to that cover as their personal turning point, the moment it all clicked for them. It's fascinating to uncover how interconnected all of this—the success, the progress, the highest of highs—truly is. It's for that reason that this community remains so powerful over a decade since *Vogue Italia*'s curve issue hit newsstands. Because together they stand, side by side with women of yesterday and activists of tomorrow, determined to never let the momentum die out.

The gates had officially been opened, and a new wave had begun. With social media now amplifying milestones in the editorial and fashion world, body-diverse photography took centerstage. No longer could she be ignored. This was her moment, *honey*!

"Girlboss" does not begin to describe those pushing to normalize size inclusivity after the dawn of social media. Less fraudulent feminism and more *The Avengers*, a group of five women banded together in 2014 to create the representation they knew the world was craving. Among them was Ashley Graham, the future queen of curves.

Ashley had begun modeling early in her adolescence, shooting catalogs internationally, even when her then teenage self had to market clothes to more voluptuous adult women. As her career expanded, so did her impact, all under the umbrella of Ford Models. But when the well-known agency shuttered their New York City curve division, Ashley and her close confidants were left to create their own opportunities.

Alongside Marquita Pring, Inga Eiriksdottir, Danielle Redman, and Julie Henderson, the five leading ladies formed ALDA—the name means "wave" in Icelandic, signaling the coming change—a collaborative effort to represent true beauty beyond archaic barriers. Armed and contoured, they presented their idea to Ivan Bart, president of IMG Models & Fashion, who, in a move that would change the future of fashion, signed them all.

The intent spoke for itself: to create a future where the conversation about "plus size versus straight size" was unnecessary. And with the backing of IMG's reputation and resources, the dream seemed more like a reality for these five trailblazers by the minute. "It makes an impact because it's breaking the segregation between straight and plus," Ashley told *Vogue Italia*. "All of IMG's top talent is [now] pooled together."

That talent now included not just women of various races, ethnicities, and backgrounds but size as well. And it wasn't enough to simply lump them all together. No, as Mina White, director at IMG, explains, it meant ensuring that every woman represented was being treated and paid both fairly and equally.

"There was power in numbers and power in telling that story," Mina says, recalling the day she first came in contact with the ladies of ALDA. "My daughter was fifteen at the time, and she'd been around supermodels her entire life, she was born into this. And this was the first time ever, after meeting the curve models, that she said to me, 'I really think that what you're doing is amazing.' And she's not plus size, but she was able to identify [with these women]. This was what was needed for us to change the fabric of how young women talk to themselves."

Mina and IMG helped the women of ALDA not only secure regular gigs but also craft a high-fashion vision for what the future could look like, and what they could achieve in their wildest dreams. And that vision was simple: equality. Just as their thin counterparts had been given, these five women wanted to change to show how marvelous they could be on set—not solely in catalogs but in the most glamorous editorials.

Ivan adds, "They were just so engaging and filled with light and energy. They were fantastic and so self-confident, and I began to understand what body positivity [truly is] and being so comfortable in your skin. The way forward was really just to have conversations and to really sell it."

As a plus-size woman herself, Mina knows firsthand how influential true representation can be. It's a fact she's reminded me of frequently nowadays, anytime one of her girls lands a magazine cover or major gig. Or even when they accomplish milestones outside fashion that remind society of their sheer humanity. A favorite moment is the day Ashley landed her legendary *Sports Illustrated* cover. It was a difficult day for Mina, her confidence at a personal low, feeling as though she had absolutely nothing to wear (the cover reveal was to be filmed and broadcast, after all). But in support, she pushed through and attended the grand moment, and it's one that will forever be cemented into her memory: witnessing Ashley break into tears reminded her of the power at her—and our—fingertips. This was more than just fashion; this was the future. And Ashley had just burst through another door.

"Ashley's comfortable in her own skin and she makes you feel comfortable," Ivan says. "The same thing goes with Paloma Elsesser and Precious Lee and Gigi Hadid. If you're a star, you have a star quality. And I think that's consistent with any top model [regardless of size]—having this ability to communicate, to be the light in the room, and to make others around you feel included and excited."

Mina adds, "Still, we're barely scratching the surface. There's so much work to be done. But I also feel really good about the work that has been done and I feel like fifteen years from now, we can look back—you, myself, all of these key people—and say that we changed an industry forever. And so I'm not going to stop doing that until I know that change has been evoked in a major way."

In the years since then, other agencies have propelled plus-size talent, too, like the Btwn, which now represents models of various races and genders up to a size 30. And what they've found is, in the years since their launch, the pool of talent to pull from has grown exponentially. A TikTok casting call they had in the early months of the COVID-19 pandemic garnered thousands of submissions a day from folk across the country. It's clear there are infinite stories waiting to be told through the most beautiful of lenses.

"We're inundated with incredible submissions with huge ranges of body types and sizes," says Jane Belfry, founder and agency director at the Btwn. "People want to feel seen, they want to participate. People are willing to put themselves out there more because of social media."

As Ashley and fellow models picked up steam, the industry divide between straight- and plus-size girls still remained. Those of larger body types were viewed as less skilled, often excluded from high fashion and the world of editorial. It's because of this that many curvy women rejected the term *plus size*, finding it to be more harmful than helpful. While thin women could select their model mode—commercial, editorial, fitness, and the like—curvy gals were sequestered into one group, dictated and limited by their size.

Various terms have emerged in an effort to reimagine *plus size*, from fat to extended to, in the words of Ashley herself, "curva-sexilicious." Yet many question why a label is needed altogether when plus sizes are the average, not the *other*.

The debate around the term *plus size* seemed foreign to me as I embarked on my first fashion week back in 2019, tasked with deconstructing the conversation for *Glamour*'s first totally plus-size digital issue. As a topic, it seemed mundane, lacking the substance to take centerfold in the (virtual) pages of the magazine. That is, until I began conducting interviews, when I instantly realized that the debate is less centered on the term, and more in the harrowing notion of internalized fatphobia.

Terminology aside, the larger issue is how these women feel the term either limits and degrades them or gives them an advantage. Both can ring true, depending on who has the stage.

For many models—particularly those of a higher status—*plus-size* minimizes their potential, excluding them from the likes of Gigi and Bella Hadid who have endless castings to choose from. Because at large (pun intended), fashion still views curvy women as less than, unable to match the level of excellence that thin models can command on a moment's notice. It doesn't matter how many Ashley Grahams walk the runway; plus size has been viewed by fashion insiders—and continues to be, in some capacity—as a roadblock, rather than an opportunity.

The term is a bit of a walking contradiction: How can a size that is the national average be "plus," or outside the norm? But until the fashion industry can cater to size inclusivity, a term like *plus size* remains vital in simplifying the shopping experience. Few frustrations match that of entering a store, finding the perfect dress, and coming to realize that, like roughly 80 percent of the fashion industry, the designer has excluded your body. *Plus size* gives shoppers a firm indicator that they are welcome, embraced, and accepted within the scope of the brand.

"You don't see people saying drop the petite or drop the tall," argues writer Liz Black. "It's just drop the plus, because to them, the term equates 'fat,' and fat equals bad."

Distaste for *plus size* belongs to the eye of the beholder. But as more and more models distance themselves from the term, is it acceptable to capitalize off the plus-size community while refusing to acknowledge yourself as such?

Throughout her career, Liz has found that those who most loudly advocate against the use of the term are on the smaller end of the size spectrum, usually donning a size between 8 and 12. Sometimes, their distaste is for good reason: Why lump them in with women of higher sizes who actually face body discrimination on a regular basis when that is not their lived experience? On the flip side, however, Liz argues that some might not want to be associated with the realm of fatness altogether, stemming from an internalized bias against larger bodies.

The term also feeds into the flawed notion that plus-size women are a singular customer, rather than a spectrum of beautiful individuals with varying tastes and body types. "The plus community is not a monolith," says Sarah Chiwaya, creator of the blog *Curvily*. "We all have different aesthetics and budgets and wants for what we need in fashion."

Sarah created the viral hashtag #PlusSizePlease in 2014 in response to her newfound love for the digital fashion community, urging others to use their platforms to directly demand that brands increase their size ranges. "Seeing plus-size people identifying as plus size, looking absolutely fly, and living their best lives was so revolutionary to me. It changed how I felt about myself in such a profound way."

That feeling of community is the strongest argument in favor of the term. It allows those who live in marginalized bodies to connect, sympathize, empathize, and support one another, bonding over the scars of how society has treated us, and the dreams for how it can be changed.

And change was imminent, with new brands like Universal Standard—founded by Alex Waldman and Polina Veksler in 2015—rising from the threads, offering clothing for women sizes 00 through 40.

"The reason that we have the largest commercially available size spectrum in the world is because we don't want to talk about size," explains Alex. "We don't care what size you are. What's important is that as a woman you have access to a style that's desirable, and that it's the kind of style that would be coveted by the smaller women who already have everything in the world to choose from."

Universal Standard mimicked the change in culture in its approach to inclusivity: free of labels, welcoming to all. Alex and Polina fought to break the binary vision of what fashion was, creating what it had the possibility to become. Rather than labeling themselves as plus-size inclusive, the brand has gravitated toward a message of "size equality," as Alex puts it.

"And not only does this work, but it works to the benefit of absolutely everyone: certainly the industry, the individual, the creative community—everyone involved benefits if we start looking at women as a group rather than a size range." That includes taking the time to understand different needs from a financial perspective, and how accessibility plays a role in what women purchase.

With top models bringing the message to the mainstream and brands starting to follow suit, the focus began to switch from the future of plus-size fashion to the future of capital *F* fashion. While the term *plus size* holds its pros and cons, the core of the conversation cannot be lost: the future that every one of these women fought for is not segregated on the basis of size but rather a level playing field for all to partake in. Because for as long as this community is viewed as the "other," we will always be the lesser.

Identifying with the terms *plus size* and *fat* felt natural to me as I embarked on my own body journey in college. The difficulty came, however, as I entered more elite fashion spaces—places that resembled *The Devil Wears Prada*, rather than more welcoming rooms in *The Bold Type*—and quickly found that pride and outspokenness in my size were not as accepted as they had been in my secluded bubbles of the Internet.

A pivotal moment came for me in 2019 when I convinced my editors at *NYLON* to commission me to write a feature interviewing twenty-six of the top voices in plus-size fashion, speaking to the progress we've made as an industry and how far we've yet to go. The feature—which ran during New York Fashion Week that September—was my first time connecting with icons who blazed the trail for my career to even exist. With free reign to select subjects without needing editor approval, I embarked on an email frenzy, chasing down the top talent in the industry in hopes of securing interviews.

The problem? At the time, the piece's original headline was set to be "Fashion's Fat Rebels," my personal invention that I felt best fit the narrative of the article: bold, powerful, and liberating for those who, in the pages of such mainstream fashion publications, had never felt embraced. Ignorant to the controversy behind the term, I realized quickly that *NYLON*'s prestige wouldn't be enough to counteract the internalized fatphobia I faced.

From publicists to agents, a handful of my top picks turned down the opportunity—unless I promised to remove the word *fat* from the article headline. Despite self-labeling themselves as advocates for our community, some—several of whom I looked up to, and still do to this day—felt uncomfortable being lumped in under the umbrella term.

I approached my supportive editor, who let me make the call here. We wouldn't be removing the word. In that moment I felt the weight of the issue on my back: give in, or stand true to what I believe, what I *know*, is right.

Choosing how to self-identify is a challenging, empowering journey. For those who embark on a path to reclaim a term that has been used as a weapon against them—like the word *fat*— reaching that level of comfortability within the language they select is blissful. For others, however, reclaiming words like *fat* is simply not desired.

In a society that constantly traps us in narrow boxes, reclaiming the power to self-identify is a bold step in one's body journey. And it is just that: a journey. Just as weight fluctuates over one's lifetime, so does how we choose to label ourselves. A woman might feel comfortable with *fat* one year and not the next. Another might like *curvy* and may have no desire to ever expand upon that. Others simply do not want to be defined by their size at all.

Whatever your choice, it should be universally supported from all sides of the community—because language is personal, language is important, and language is a reflection of who we are at our core.

The issue that has risen in recent years, however, is a powerful impulse to police one's chosen descriptors. Those who don't feel comfortable with using the term *fat* are sometimes viewed as lesser along on their body journeys, harboring an internalized discomfort with their size. Others feel they need to get überspecific about labels, using expressions like *visibly plus size*—meaning, higher on the size spectrum—and *midsize*—meaning, between sizes 8 and 12—to qualify their ability to speak on personal experiences. For many, myself included, it all begins to feel divisive.

If, at the core of this community, we center the topic of personal choice, why is that not always respected when it comes to comfortability?

I don't blame those models for turning down the opportunity to be in my feature that September. On the contrary, I deeply appreciate their honesty because I now understand the pressure on *their* shoulders. It's one thing to proudly claim your size and fatness in private. It's another to speak out about it in an industry that might chastise you for doing so.

Many struggle to understand the complexity of that issue. If a top model self-selects *fat* over *curvy*, they may be viewed as less palatable by the industry. It may prevent them from going on to be the next supermodel, the next brand ambassador, the next Ellen. *Curvy* may be able to get them there. And when landing in that top-level position, they still, despite not identifying with *fat*, would be breaking the beauty ideal for a new audience. Progress? Yes. But at what cost? At the cost of the community feeling that they've been sold out, capitalized on? Will they understand why you've distanced yourself from their terminology? That is the eternal question.

The trouble with being an innovator is balancing the public pressure placed upon you to use your platform for more than just your own benefit. One wrong move and you can harm a community. One slip of the tongue and suddenly, those who once identified with your voice feel ostracized by it. Especially when being the first to break down barriers, as most of these super-models were, navigating the new and rapidly shifting playing field and the implications that come with every little step is a messy task. Some, like myself, can speak out loudly with minimal fear of retaliation as our livelihoods don't depend on brand collaborations and sponsorships. Others are not as fortunate. Publicly claiming their fatness may mean fewer bookings, fewer opportunities to break the beauty ideal.

Perhaps the real issue is that the need for a chapter dedicated to terminology still exists. If a debate remains on how to label ourselves from within the community, how can we expect those outside to understand the various complexities at play? It's the twenty-first century, after all. Are labels still a necessity? Perhaps my very writing here is feeding into a narrative not all will agree or align with. Perhaps it's far more interconnected than we all understand.

Still, I'll never regret my decision to stick firmly to the term *fat*. Because looking back, it set the tone for the journalist I so desperately aspired to be. One who spoke truth, who spoke fire, who made people uncomfortable in the best way. A journalist on a mission to save lives and liberate others from the purgatory of fatphobia. I felt so emboldened by writers like Aubrey Gordon of the Internet persona Your Fat Friend, who not only used but also reclaimed the word in powerful ways.

There's true power in taking back agency from the very thing weaponized against you.

4

CURSE OF THE TOKEN
CURVE GIRL

Hunter McGrady will never forget the moment she first quit modeling.

"I showed up on set to a T-shirt job," she recalls, "and the casting team stood up, looked at me kind of sideways, and turned me away. They said, 'Wow, we didn't realize how big you were.'"

Hunter was a size 2.

At sixteen she felt fully prepared to follow in the footsteps of her mother, Brynja, who had previously reached a level of success in the modeling world. But time and time again, from casting agents and industry insiders, Hunter was told that she was not enough. Or rather, that she was *too* much, and needed to shrink down to a 00 before being worthy of the camera. "I was led to believe that being too big was the worst thing ever."

Little did she know that a decade later, she'd become *Sports Illustrated*'s curviest model to ever grace the pages of their Swimsuit issue.

With modeling on the back burner, teenage Hunter assumed a nannying job as she rethought ways to tackle the world of entertainment and fashion. All of that changed when, a few years later, she'd come across *Vogue Italia*'s legendary curve issue. "I saw it and thought, 'These are the three most beautiful women I've ever seen in my entire life, and they actually look like me.'"

That moment remains ingrained in Hunter's memory to this day: "I can tell you what I was wearing, where I was sitting, what I was thinking—everything." It opened her eyes to the world of plus-size modeling, and the potential available for a woman with a larger, growing frame. Signing with a major agency soon after, it all suddenly made sense: Hunter hadn't abandoned modeling at sixteen out of fear or failure. The industry just wasn't ready for her excellence quite yet. Two weeks later she flew to Miami for her first job: the catwalk of Miami Swim Week.

Suddenly, Hunter was everywhere, appearing in campaigns for brands like Forever 21, Macy's, and Nordstrom. All of it led up to Hunter's career-defining first spread within *Sport Illustrated*'s Swimsuit issue in 2016.

With Ashley Graham on the cover, Hunter was in great company. When showing up to set, there was no concern of whether the swimsuits pulled would fit her. Rather, Hunter was to be nude, illuminated in body paint. And thankfully, rather than feeling exposed or oversexualized, Hunter felt embraced. She wasn't nude because that was simply the only way to shoot her curves. She was nude because she wanted to be, and because it meant so much for her younger self.

"That was so liberating for me because I knew at that moment that this was going to be momentous. How awesome would it have been when I was younger if I was able to open a magazine and see someone who looked like me? I think it would have saved me."

That issue of *Sports Illustrated* put Hunter on the map, and made way for a new era of body positivity at the magazine. But the high was short lived. "I had just come off the shoot and I looked so great, I felt great. I did press for three months for that and thought, 'Shoot, this is insane.' Now all the while, my agent at the time was telling me, 'You've got to lose weight if you want to continue working as a plus-size model.'"

Once again, Hunter was just "too big."

Hunter stood firm in her stance on body acceptance, refusing to lose weight or shrink down to fit an ideal as she first felt pressured to at sixteen. Her then agent warned her that despite the *Sports Illustrated* success her client list would evaporate overnight if she didn't abide by their rules.

"And guess what? It did. I went from a size 14/16 to a size 18, and I lost 90 percent of my clients because I wasn't the 'perfect plus.'"

She adds, "It was a real point of contention for me, because here I am in this industry where it's all about body positivity and loving your body, and all the while on the back end of things—the things that people don't see and don't hear—I'm being told to change. It was a really bizarre juxtaposition."

Hunter was essentially presented with two choices: lose weight and make money or stay how you are and do what's right. She chose the latter.

The concept of the "perfect plus" or "acceptable plus body" has created a new, unattainable ideal for many women—big breasts, small waist, and the Kardashian-esque hourglass figure. Designers have gravitated toward only representing that palatable version of plus, one that *slightly* pushes the boundaries but that's not *too* fat for comfort, by exclusively casting size 12/14 models. And these models, while spectacular in their own right, hardly represent the average plus-size woman.

Hunter's firm dedication to inclusivity across the aisle is what's made her a leading advocate in the space. She refuses to back down, even when that might mean major financial loss. At fashion week in September of 2019, she turned down over thirty jobs that didn't meet her inclusivity standard.

"Showcase women of all sizes, all heights, all ranges," Hunter says. "Showcase women with larger midsections. Showcase women that have no boobs, that are all hips. Showcase different bodies and design for that. Now, *that's* impressive."

The "perfect plus" is a prime example of how far the industry still has to go. Because if fashion's version of body diversity is yet another impossibly proportioned ideal, then how much progress has actually been made?

The gravitation toward the "perfect plus" stems from many sources. For starters, sample sizes. Just as with straight-size gals, designers create sample sizes for their models to walk in. A size 12/14 has become the sweet spot for designers as it showcases a curvier body without pushing the boundaries too far, or requiring more attention, detail, and money dedicated to nailing fit.

As more weight is added to the body, more variation in sizes becomes necessary. From apple to pear shape, each woman may hold their weight differently, especially as they pass a size 18. This allows for more variety, which from a designer's standpoint lends itself to increasing complications. Whereas creating a sample size 18 or above would allow for more diverse body types to be represented, it would require more work from a designer's perspective: fitting, tailoring, and all the rest. And for designers on a time crunch leading up to fashion week, many simply don't want to take the plunge.

Instead, they create size 12/14 sample sizes each season with specific curve models in mind, knowing exactly how to fit for that specific woman's body. It's the easy route out, Hunter explains. You get the press and pat on the back for including curvy bodies without actually pushing the boundaries in a monumental way. All of it can begin to weigh on a model's mind quickly. In an industry so deeply dictated by your physical appearance, navigating work with mental health is a difficult balance.

"It's an interesting dichotomy for the very thing that caused my insecurity, my anxiety, and my depression to become the reason for my success in the career that I love," says model Allie Weber.

That's especially true when social media trolls attack with vicious hatred. It feels like an impossible battle, one with little hope for escape.

"When you already have spent most of your life thinking that you're less than because you're fat, when strangers on the Internet now feel comfortable telling you that, that was really hard the first time it happened," Allie recalls. "It's the nameless, faceless people on the Internet hiding behind the screen, because they don't see models as people; they see them as public figures."

Throughout my career, I've noticed an unsettling trend in how major publications cover body diversity—almost always in a positive light. They reinforce capitalism's co-opting of body positivity, watering down the life-altering movement into a trendy catchphrase. And when it comes time to hold brands accountable for their shortcomings, they fall short in doing so. They claim these brands are "making an effort" when, in reality, that effort is a misguided bare minimum.

And while it is, of course, necessary to celebrate the major wins and milestones, failing to reflect on the shortcomings of this industry, and the leaps and bounds we've yet to tackle, does a grand disservice to those, like Hunter, who are actively advocating for change every day, even when it means the loss of a paycheck. Purposefully spotlighting the highlights will never move the needle in the way we so desperately crave.

"People still don't know where to put us, and people don't think we're marketable, which is wild because more people look like us than what is the 'acceptable' plus body," says Jordan Underwood (they/he), a New York City–based model who falls on the higher end of the size spectrum.

Jordan has undergone the gamut of uncomfortable on-set experiences, like once when, surrounded by size 16 models, they were told to head home for the day at 10:00 AM, despite being booked for a full eight hours. When the campaign launched, not one image of Jordan—who wore a size 24 at the time—was used.

"It was very indicative to me of the ways in which the industry is so resistant to anything that deviates, to the point where they won't even take the pictures. They won't even see what could happen. . . . More consumers want to see the change than the people who are making the decisions. Sometimes their sense of self is so inflated that they forget that their job, under capitalism, is because people pay for these clothes."

The experience is twofold for Jordan. On one end, it's difficult to land major gigs as a size 24 model. On the other, they find themselves stuck in a battle with the gender binary that, despite fashion's faux inclusivity smokescreen, remains central to the modeling world. At large, agency websites remain divided into "men" and "women" sections. The plus-size sector specifically remains hyperfeminine.

"A lot of times, I just have to pretend that I'm a girl for the day. And it especially sucks because people on set are really, really horrible about transphobia and misgendering, and not taking into account the microaggressions that they're using."

They add, "People are so willing to use marginalized people if it helps their profit or supports their brand, but they're not willing to do the work to make sure that they're hiring people who are going to treat us properly."

Too fat. Too femme. Too masculine. Too Black. Too *other*. Find any model who deviates from the "perfect plus" ideal, and they're likely to unpack a painful plethora of stories caused by those statements.

Similar is true for Lydia Okello, a nonbinary model based in Canada. Although their experience in the industry has veered more positively, navigating tricky and unpleasant on-set interactions has served as a reminder that their body is not yet embraced in the way the media paints it to be.

"Feeling that sort of trepidation, or even perceiving a bit of frustration because my body can't pose the same way as a straight-size model can," Lydia says. "That learning curve of photographers who are used to shooting very thin, almost six foot tall people, now having to adjust the way that they work for somebody who has a different body shape and size—in my experience, there's definitely quite a few photographers who maybe are out of their depth in that way."

They add, "It doesn't mean that we can't make really beautiful work or fulfill what you're hoping to fulfill. But it's different. And I think we're still really working on people understanding that and getting the education on the way that it's different to shoot plus models."

The discomfort falls on the model, then, who is forced to push past that awkward energy on set and perform their best, despite an ambiance that does not lend itself to that type of excellence. But if photographers, creative directors, and other industry professionals don't do their due diligence beforehand to understand fatter and nonstandard confirming bodies, why is the fault never theirs? It's a large part of the reason the same plus-size models are used time and time again: photographers and designers become comfortable with one specific woman, knowing exactly how to maneuver her curves to best "flatter" the camera. And instead of pushing themselves to go further, to represent more women, to truly emphasize the importance of diversity, they stop there.

They draw the line at the token curve girl.

For models like Lydia, it feels like a never-ending cycle. Instead of pushing to be a size 6, models are pressured to be the size 14 version of the same Western beauty ideals that have been upheld for decades. It creates this secondary feeling of inadequacy, an eternal wondering of when you can finally be deemed acceptable.

Lydia adds, "With the very little representation that fat folks are getting, it's still perpetuating the idea that there's a right way to look."

And the lengths the modeling industry will go to promote that ideal are beyond dangerous. Perhaps the most common method is through padding, the fashion world's Build-A-Bear method at transforming curvy bodies into unattainable, manufactured vessels for public desire.

When Hanna (a pseudonym), a now popular curve model, first entered the industry, she nearly fit the "perfect plus" ideal. The second that switched, however, and her figure began to deviate from that approved state, her agent introduced the topic of padding. Like a more glamorous version of a fat suit, padding allows models to fit into sample sizes that are bigger than their actual frames. It is often used to enhance certain body features, emphasizing the hourglass figure or Kardashian-like butt and thighs. Despite trepidation, trusting that her agent knew best, Hanna eventually obliged and began padding.

In her experience, however, like other models who requested to speak anonymously on the topic, the fault lies less in the hands of casting directors and more in those of agents who do their utmost to present clients they believe will be best marketable to brands. They push and push for their clients to fulfill a near-impossible checklist of what it takes to be the perfect curve girl. And any deviation is seen as a betrayal.

Because at the end of the day, everything is about money. More bookings means more money in the agent's pockets. Brands now have infinite amounts of curve girls to choose from, but an agent only has so many on their roster to meet their personal financial quota.

And that's where the padding comes in. Too small for this brand? No worries, just pad up! Can't fit the sample size? No problem, simply slip into this. Fool the women at home into believing you're *this* beautiful, when in reality, none of it is real.

"It's a really flawed concept," Hanna says. "With padding, you can only pad so much. You can't pad your arms. You can't pad your collarbones. A lot of it falls on the agent because they think, 'Oh, my God, *this* is where the money is. This is the only way we should market people.' When in reality, that's not the case. And I find so many girls have had more success when they're able to be themselves."

She adds, "It's not rocket science. It's models."

Padding not only does a disservice to the consumers who are now further affected by this unattainable body ideal but also throws the very models on set through a dangerous loop, which Hanna describes as an "unbelievably frustrating" scenario.

"So how I am as I am, is not sufficient for you," she says. "And you try not to take it personally, but it's demoralizing, it's degrading. And it got to the point where I just refused to do it because I just thought it was unacceptable, and it made me feel so horrible."

Never mind their personality or face or what they bring to the table. In those moments, these models are reduced down to simply their size. And no matter what they do, unless they can fit the new fat ideal, they are deemed not worthy. For a subset of the industry that claims to promote body positivity and self-love, that feels like the very antithesis of the message.

Kris Yeo, a Canadian plus-size model, feels similar. At the start of her career circa 2009, she felt uncomfortable in front of the camera, especially when surrounded by mostly thin models. It was the rare moments of sisterhood that helped her build her confidence, like one time when shooting for Kohls when none other than Ashley Graham—who was also shooting that day—jumped on set to help encourage a young Kris to be her true authentic self.

But that authenticity only gets you so far when the industry is constantly working against you.

"Honestly, I have PTSD now from a tape measure," Kris says. "I've had agents telling me that they want me to get liposuction on my hips. If you were a 14/16, that was pushing it. And then if you were a size 12/14, you were too small. Because my measurements on paper read 'too big,' we would have to dumb down my bra size because we didn't want to scare the clients."

All of it came crashing down when a former agent instructed Kris to lose weight in order to fit that more standard size 14 that brands were often gravitating toward. She obliged. But soon she had lost *too* much weight. Because of her natural hourglass figure, pounds had shed off in the "wrong" areas, causing her to be pressured into padding.

"I felt like I was lying. Why can't I just have my normal body? It only adds on like two inches. How is that going to read differently in photos?"

She adds, "I would be pumping up these women [seeing these campaigns], but really behind the shadows, I was feeling like shit, because I was getting in trouble for what my body looked like."

Weight fluctuates, even for models. But leeway or room for deviation was hardly ever part of the conversation. Kris recalls one experience in particular, when after gaining a few pounds, her then agents told her that her go-to client no longer wanted to book her. She had simply gotten too fat for them.

Imagine her shock when, soon after, that very client began messaging her directly, saying they were attempting to book her but were suddenly not hearing back . . . from the agents. "I felt like I was being punished by my agency for gaining weight."

On set, however, she found solace from other (thinner, straight-size) models, who, unlike photographers and agents of the time, would express their love for curvier bodies, and desire to have Kris's natural features. It became the strangest dichotomy: the media had painted models as being competitive and backstabbing when really they were perhaps the only ones uplifting one another.

The modeling space as a whole often only feels welcoming when you fit neatly into one category. Choose from the list of identities and maybe, just maybe, you'll be deemed worthy of having a seat at the table. But if you exist somewhere between multiple intersections, far too often the doors remain closed. For plus-size hopefuls, that means the boundary has already been laid; your body is the obstacle to overcome. Add on another "difficulty"—like gender, ethnicity, disability—and you're disqualified from the race.

Well, screw that.

"On social media, women like me or people who look like me, we are all categorized as Instagram models, but we're not categorized as supermodels," says Saucyé West, one of the most outspoken voices in the industry. "When you [look at the models of today], there's no variation of size, height, weight. They all look the same, even white and racially ambiguous."

Saucyé is unapologetically candid for a reason: because too few are willing to speak up. Even at the cost of a paycheck or major booking, she is the first to call out foolery, constantly starting and continuing major conversations that echo throughout the halls of the fashion industry.

Saucyé lives at the intersection of multiple marginalizations, existing in a visibly fat, dark-skinned Black body. At times, when piled high one above the other, her identities are turned against her, silencing her with the label of being just another "angry Black woman." But in conversation, in emotional and deep moments, you quickly begin to realize why she is the trailblazer so many aspire to be: Because she views her identities as her superpower.

The difference between Saucyé and many of her colleagues in the industry is their attitude toward the conversation of body politics, because for someone like Saucyé, their very livelihood is inherently political. Each and every move she makes is informed, if not dictated, by the political oppression she faces.

"White, plus-size influencers do not want to say Black models are being treated badly. I have not heard one White, plus-size successful model call that mess out," she says. "I think that once they start saying that, then we can start moving forward, the conversation can happen. But if they're not saying anything, that's way more damaging."

She adds, "Everyone's comfortable, everyone's getting their bag. And I'm just like, 'Is getting a bag more important than seeing the movement go forward?'"

All of it points to the topic of performative activism. In our social media–first culture, "uplifting" or "amplifying" diverse voices has increasingly become a commercialized trend, a method often used by brands and influencers to cover their bases and appear to be supportive when behind the scenes their efforts are laughable. It's a topic Saucyé is well versed in from her personal experience. Online, many are quick to share her posts and Twitter threads, painting the picture of unity from behind the screen. But when it comes time for tangible action, their efforts stop at the "share" feature. She explains that many of those who exclaim "Inclusivity!" online are the very ones supporting brands that are actively working against those who, like Saucyé, can't even get the time of day.

What does it mean to be a leader in the plus-size space if your very platform is centered in self, rather than community liberation and acceptance?

"As a Black woman, I'm tired of continuously yelling, fighting, and being called bitter and angry," says Leah Vernon, a model and author of the book *Unashamed: Musings of a Fat, Black Muslim*. "In this business, it's about how many eyes are on you. It's not necessarily about the quality of your work. And so just because I was born and shaped a certain kind of way, doesn't mean that I should get less exposure or less money and less opportunities."

From the outside, Leah has accomplished it all: a successful modeling career, a book deal, a popular and rising platform. But behind the scenes, like so many others, she is constantly toiling with the bigotry this industry throws at her each step of the way.

As a fat, Black, Muslim woman in the mainstream world, Leah has often experienced tokenization. It's a difficult minefield to navigate. On one hand, being the first in many situations has allowed her to open doors that may have remained shut if she did not persist. On the other, she is used and capitalized off for the very things that make her a target in today's world. The conversation then skews less on what Leah can accomplish as a model and more on how she can make a designer or brand look good in the public eye.

And on set, those subliminal messages begin to seep deep below the surface. For Leah, constantly being the biggest on set, being the most "othered," has fueled her battle with body dysmorphia. "Where are the other models that look like me? I know that they exist, I talk to them every day."

And why aren't they hired?

Tokenization runs rampant through the fashion industry today. All of it feels like a checklist: Have a fat model? Great. A Black one? Great! A disabled one? Even better. But all that is, all that's accomplished through tokenization, is crumbs.

"And I'm not excited for crumbs, I never will be," Leah says. "It's exhausting every day to have to continually prove myself in this industry, . . . [but] as usual, Black woman comes to the rescue, to carry the fucking goddamn world on her back with nothing in return."

Also tokenized and hardly represented are those of the Asian American and Pacific Islander community, largely because of assumptions around what Asian women look like.

"They always think Asian women are so skinny, that we're shy," says influencer Scarlett Hao. "Those are stereotypes, and it takes a long time to educate them on the fact that there's a big population of plus-size people in Asia."

Originally from China, Scarlett has found the plus-size fashion community's wins bittersweet considering the sheer lack of Asian representation. She feels as though her culture is greatly undervalued within this space, and that little room is made for her stories and others like it.

Ushshi Rahman, a Bangladeshi writer, agrees. "I think American media and people have to understand that there's really room for everybody," Ushshi says. "And not only that, but it's a necessity to be able to tell as much of everybody's experience. When we tell stories, when we include people in the media, when we start to make room for this, we grant and allow for more freedom for all people. Because when you see yourself represented in the larger narrative, you then have more personal power as well."

All of it can begin to feel hopeless. Leave the industry and suddenly, those trickled—and yes, tokenized—moments of inclusivity evaporate, perhaps to never be seen again. Or stay, keep fighting, keep enduring, keep pushing, at the risk of your own sanity and well-being.

What drives women like Leah is, once again, the community.

Few things make sense in the fashion industry. Few things seem rational enough to be real, to take full form. Few things feel worth the fight. But for plus-size women, the answer is always community. Because all of it—the bigotry, the hatred, the pain—all of it is a shared experience. It is the connector that lives between all of us, that binds us in ways nearly unexplainable. Because in those shared moments of pain, of torture, of "other," we suddenly are never alone.

When the community is centered, everything is possible. Success is possible. Change—real change—is possible. But it's when that begins to fade—when agents take over, when models distance themselves from the very women who uplifted them, when they reject and ridicule terms like *fat*, why they fail to pay Black, marginalized women their dues—all hell breaks loose. Those are the moments when that communal power is more important than ever. Because without it, who could ever endure—who could even *want* to endure—the injustices of the modeling world?

"I want to create those moments in the community of people just feeling free," Saucyé says. "I just want us to be free and do whatever the hell we want to with our bodies without feeling ashamed and scared."

That is what we're fighting for.

COMMUNITY, CONVERSATION, AND CHANGE

WITH COMMUNITY COMES POWER. Power to enact change on a personal and professional level. If there's one lesson I've learned in my time as a journalist, it's that fashion must be changed from the inside out. That means giving a seat at the table for those whose voices are rarely reflected, and in some cases, creating our own tables from the ground up.

CeCe Olisa, Katie Sturino, and Kristine Thompson are phenomenal examples of that. As cocreator of the CurvyCon—an annual convention for plus-size shoppers—CeCe's work is driven by the transformative power of feeling included. Katie's personal experiences led her to launching Megababe, an anti–thigh chafing brand that has revolutionized women and provided never-before-had comfort on an everyday basis. And Kristine's experiences as a top style influencer culminated in her own fashion line, KIN by Kristine, which gave this shopper something she desperately craved: trendy clothing.

Together, these three women breathe life into the topic of community and how brands can better serve, market, and provide for us.

This conversation has been edited for clarity and length.

In what ways have you seen this community change the fashion industry as a whole from the inside out, on both a business and personal level?

Kristine Thompson: I don't feel like these brands would have ever turned the page towards size-inclusivity if it wasn't for the constant calling out, bringing attention to, highlighting, and rallying around that this community did for years. That is what helped make this much more of a universally, not only accepted, but demanded type of thing.

CeCe Olisa: Plus-size women taught me body positivity and self-love. This community taught me to love my body when I came into it from a place of insecurity. That type of lesson—to really embrace yourself holistically at any size, whether it's in a workout class, in the fitting room, on your wedding day—is a massive, life-changing lesson.

Katie Sturino: The reason I started my brand or even felt like I had space to do that was by reading the comments of other women who liked seeing my body size represented in a fashion blog. That makes you feel less alone, and it makes you feel less shameful, like there actually might be a chance that you could band together to make change.

What misconceptions do you think brands still have regarding plus-size shoppers?

KS: They don't think that plus-size women want to spend money. They don't think plus-size women want to look nice. They think we want to hide, and they assume that this is our temporary body.

KT: I think the number-one misconception is that brands think we don't like fashion trends and that we don't want the same thing that our thin counterparts have. It's a vicious cycle. Brands will try to do something that's trendier, but they don't put the same effort and energy and resources behind it as they would their straight-size line.

CO: Brands underestimate how confident plus-size women can be. There's a desire for style and to be on-trend that I think that some brands just don't see. So much of being a plus-size woman is emotional. There's a concrete understanding of what the world says about curvy bodies, and I think that there is a very deep and painful rejection in the fitting room when clothes don't fit. But when you find a place that makes you feel accepted, especially through fashion, it's that much more sweet.

Kristine, what has launching your own brand, KIN by Kristine, taught you about this customer?

KT: I am also that woman and customer, so it has just confirmed what I always thought. As a collective, we can all say that we want better quality clothing. I have been on this side of plus all of my adult life, so I know what makes me feel good in clothing, and I just want to continue to offer that to women.

And Katie, for you, what has it been like to bring Megababe to life?

KS: Magical and incredible and unbelievable. Before I started Megababe, I just wanted something that was going to solve thigh chafing in my life that wasn't embarrassing or made for men or athletes. And I was shocked that there was nothing on the market that was cool or clean. It's interesting to launch a product that people say changed their life. Some women say, "This changed the way I dress in the summer," or "I feel confident now walking around because I know I'm not going to be in pain." So there's this impact that I've been able to have with different people that has been really life changing for me.

For brands that want to take the dive into plus, how do you think they can better serve us? What steps can they take to best tackle this market and provide options for our community?

CO: The leadership of brands does not reflect the end consumer. If people who don't look like the community start making decisions for the community, there's a lot that gets lost in translation. Plus-size women could be served with much more specificity and much more success if actual plus-size women were the decision makers that were helping bring these brands to life.

KT: I think the most important thing is having someone who is plus size on the fit team, or someone who can at least reach out to a diverse group of bodies within the plus-size community to have meetings and consultations, and to have them involved during your development process. Because otherwise, it's very apparent to us as the consumer who has invested time in fitting on plus-size bodies—and a variety of them, not just one shape— and who has not.

KS: No brand should be putting out a collection above a size extra large without talking to a woman who is above a size extra large. That's where brands so often get it wrong by having the same type of people in one room talking about a community and how to make clothes for them who aren't actually represented in that room. And I find that that happens a shocking amount of the time.

What does the inclusive future of fashion look like to you?

KT: Rihanna said it best: you can never be inclusive enough. We need to stop only highlighting a certain type of plus and really expose the community for what it truly is: we all have different types of bodies and hold our weight in different ways, and one is not better than the other.

KS: Support brands that are actually investing in plus. We need to give companies a little bit of grace as they're expanding into this space; Give them a bit of time to get it right.

CO: I think it's important for us to continue to talk about the curvy and plus-size experience from a sense of positivity and productivity moving forward. For a long time, this narrative of a plus-size woman was very sad and wasn't celebratory. But if you come to the CurvyCon, you see that there's so much joy to be had. My brand is built on my mantra: *Don't wait on your weight to live the life you want.* The more that we as a community articulate our lives out loud, and the more that we don't hide—and I say that as someone who started off as an anonymous blogger—the more we step out, we liberate other people.

5

THE BODY BOOM

M IDDLE AMERICA: The hidden sister. The mythical "silent majority." The *average* American woman. If the past few years of out-of-touch media have taught us anything, it's that few truly understand *who she is*. And moreover, how to reach her.

That's especially true in the plus-size fashion space, where an emphasis is placed on the New York City and Los Angeles coastal consumers. But statistics show that a majority of curvy shoppers live beyond the metropolitan boundaries, where fashion week remains a fantasy and Target shopping a lifestyle. To our everywoman, conversations around fat liberation and size equality may seem as foreign as farm life does to city dwellers. All she may know about body positivity is that the Ashley Grahams of the world are finally starting to get the recognition they deserve. Out of touch or out of reach? I lean toward the latter.

Weeks before the start of the world-shattering COVID-19 pandemic, I made the move from my birth home of New York to the Grand Canyon State, Arizona. Sometimes a desert paradise and others like the deepest pits of hell come summer, everything was new: the landscape, the shopping, the attitudes, *the people*. It dawned on me in my brief shopping adventures before the start of the pandemic that through the aisles of Macy's, Torrid, and Lane Bryant stood a plus-size woman that still awaited her time to shine, to speak. No one had told her yet that it was okay to wear a bikini, to show skin, to throw away the cold shoulder tops and peplum skirts.

And a whole wave of warriors has been doing the work to change that.

The statistic that over 68 percent of American women are plus-size gets thrown around often with little acknowledgment of who exactly those women are and how best designers, brands, and the media can serve, communicate with, and inspire them. While influencers with hundreds of thousands of followers may take the spotlight, it is the uncurated and sometimes faceless profiles pumping up their follower counts, sharing their photos, and raising their engagement rates that fuel each step of the movement. And it's about time that she—*you*—gets the attention she deserves.

With magazines of the early and mid-2000s—which, at that time, served as the tastemakers and trendsetters for the world—refusing to promote curves, the industry's then little sister, social media, would have to step up to the plate. And few could expect how powerful Internet virality would become.

That digital touch is crucial in other countries as well, particularly where the mainstream media has yet to catch up to the burgeoning conversation. Who's to tell my large Italian ancestors scattered throughout Italy that they don't need to lose weight to be beautiful without Instagram present to feed them the message? The industry's body boom could never have occurred without social media stepping in as the middleman between average women and their newfound spokespeople. While magazine-documented runways may convince you that only one or two curvy models exist, social media has thrown more than the same handful of names into the mix of women who could never quite crack the fashion industry's gate code but had life-changing stories to tell. Among them is Tess Holliday.

Mississippi-born Tess has a profound life story, one you can devour in her own book, *The Not So Subtle Art of Being a Fat Girl*. Her perseverance through tragic moments is only one of the many reasons she resonates with so many women across state and international borders. Because if anyone can show the true power of determination and authenticity, it's Tess.

Early on, Tess's passion for fashion was constrained by the trauma of her youth, not to mention the bullying she endured year after year as a young fat girl growing up in a thin-first world. But her flame was never extinguished, just hidden, waiting for its time to illuminate the perfect trail for Tess to blaze forward. Her deeply rooted artistry first led her to becoming a makeup artist, though that would soon change after making the move to Los Angeles in 2010.

Ironically enough, Tess's first on-set job was for an A&E weight loss series. "They shot me from a seven-foot-tall ladder above me to make me look wider," she recalls. "And they covered up many tattoos, they gave me bang extensions, and I remember the hair and makeup person kind of asking me like, 'How did you get this job?'"

That gig was a big deal. Not only was it for a major network but it was also run by the team who shot promotional posters for the Harry Potter series—"So that's what I cared about!" Tess jokes. Christina Aguilera was in the studio above shooting for her album. All of it pointed to Tess's face soon being plastered across the country. And despite not promoting the messaging she aligns with today—the one-season series painted obesity as a plague—it gave her the facial notoriety to launch the platform she—and we—always needed.

Soon after, Tess became a finalist in Torrid's House of Dreams Model Search, igniting the start of her soon-to-be illustrious career. And all of it stemmed from putting herself online.

In 2013 she created #EffYourBeautyStandards, a digital movement traced back to a single unplanned hashtag. Its near-instant
virality showed Tess the power that laid at her fingertips, how
with the post of a photo she could change the life of a woman
out there—in Arkansas, New York, Wisconsin, Chicago, and Mis-
souri—who so desperately wanted to feel worthy, to feel seen.

But the love was met with equal—or larger—amounts of hate.

"I immediately was met online by folks telling me you can't
wear that, you shouldn't wear that," Tess recalls. "And I just
remember thinking, *What the fuck?* I didn't even know that it
was OK to love myself, so finally figuring out that I could love
myself and I could express myself with clothing, that felt good to
me. And then having people tell me you can't or shouldn't wear
that, I just remember thinking, *Fuck that*. Like, *This is stupid*."

Navigating the trolls and triumphs of social media is a battle I
can hardly fathom. The occasional "stop promoting obesity" comments I receive on my various articles are no match for the visceral
hatred women like Tess experience on a regular basis. In many
ways, however, those trolls have only boosted plus-size models,
unknowingly lifting their voices to a wider audience. Because the
louder they scream, the more popular these trailblazers become.

#EffYourBeautyStandards was pivotal for many reasons. Used
over five million times in the years since 2013, #EffYourBeauty-
Standards became the little-hashtag-that-could, uniting women
across lines and barriers that previously prevented their voices
from being recognized. At the helm of all of it was Tess, collecting
their voices to bring to the industry, to sets, to brands in ways
that had never quite been done before.

The power of #EffYourBeautyStandards became most clear to
Tess when she was in Australia hosting a meet-and-greet. It's a
story she's told a thousand times, but one that perfectly captures

the extent of her message, and the transformative, life-altering power that comes with true self-acceptance.

After waiting in line for three hours, a middle-aged woman, accompanied by her young son, approached Tess and informed her that she'd changed her life. The year prior, the woman's older son had passed away. In planning his funeral, she discovered no photos of them together, "because she hated [her body] so much that she didn't want to be in photos," Tess recalls. "She said that it was finding me and following me that made her realize that she didn't want to do that again with her younger son." The woman showed Tess a photo of her on the beach in a bathing suit with her younger son and said that never again will she make the same mistake.

We spend so much of our lives obsessed with our bodies: how we perceive them, how they make others perceive us. We let our insecurities stop us from living to the fullest, from being the best we can be. And sometimes, it takes the world crashing down to realize that none of that matters. Not the stretch marks, the cellulite, the double chin, the jiggle and the bounce. The longer we put our lives on hold because of our size, the longer we stop ourselves from reaching happiness. And no one deserves that.

I wish I could say I practice what I preach with ease. But it's *hard*. The amount of times I've bowed out of photos, knowing that I'll hate the result. The amount of times I've rushed out of the bathroom after a shower before the mist can clear, hoping to avoid having to see my body in the mirror. The amount of times I've imagined just taking a pair of scissors and cutting my fat right off. The days I wondered if anyone could ever love me, tolerate me, at my current size. For years I wondered if life in this body is worth the stress.

That's why Tess's work matters. It's why *all* of these women do. Because in our darkest moments, in our deepest days of self-hatred, we can turn to them for the sheer hope we need to stay afloat. They are more than our spokespeople—they are often our lifelines.

Then and now, as she tells me the story of this brave Australian woman, Tess is "a bucket of tears." A mother of two herself, "I can't imagine . . . having no memories with the child that you've lost. To me, that's the sole reason why I do what I do, because it's definitely not for me. It's for others to see themselves and just know that it's OK to exist."

Who knew a hashtag could start such a personal, life-altering movement?

The role of a spokesperson is not to center their own desires or opinions but rather to accurately—as best as possible—capture the voices of their audience. Women like Tess have done so in monumental ways, and it's why many still look to them to lead the charge for change. Because while Sally in Louisiana may have no direct contact to Torrid, Tess, on the other hand, does, and she can best serve as the way to communicate the most valuable consumer feedback available.

Bigoted Internet trolls are no match for the transformative power of authenticity, as Tess and others like her have witnessed firsthand. Perhaps the only thing that can bog down that joy is critique, criticism, and anger from within the community. While bright and beautiful from the outside, the plus-size community is made of vastly different people, all with different opinions on what constitutes true inclusivity, true advocacy. Beyond the surface, below the hems and stitches, lie heated conversations on who's given a platform as a spokesperson and how they decide to use it.

Much of the problem lies in the term *inclusive* itself. Because while a brand expanding to a size 3X may double its original range of offerings, it still, despite positive efforts, neglects a portion of the community who wear above a size 24. Influencers who promote and work with these brands are sometimes accused of selling out those larger fat women for a paycheck, capitalizing on "body positivity" as a trend or buzzword while not actually moving the needle forward. Frustrations have begun to bubble over in the community as after a decade online, many advocates are simply fed up. Why, after so many years and movements and never-ending conversations are brands refusing to cater to *all*, not just *some*, plus-size folk?

Before jumping into the thick of it, it's important to note the various labels that fat activists have created to discuss the inner workings of the plus-size community as a whole:

Midsize: Those who fall below the size of an average American woman (16/18) but who, until recently, were never reflected in the fashion industry. Usually, these women fall between a size 8 and 12.

Small Fat: Those who wear a 1X–2X, size 18 and lower.

Midfat: Those who wear a size 2X–3X, size 20 to 24.

Super Fat: Those who wear a size 4X–5X, size 26 to 32.

Infinifat: Those who wear a size 6X or 32 and higher.

And when a sole individual is granted spokesperson status by a brand or designer to speak for the spectrum listed above, chaos erupts.

In mid-2021 I embarked on my first fashion event since the start of the pandemic: an intimate dinner in Los Angeles to celebrate the launch of a new brand that, at the time, catered to wearers up to a size 22 with plans to expand quickly. I attended as a journalist, not paid influencer or guest, covering a story about the power of community. Little did I know the backlash that would soon occur in the coming days.

As images and videos circled social media in the days following the event, some spoke out in anger that so many from within the community—particularly top industry names—publicly supported a brand that left out super- and infinifats (though the attendees did reflect a wide spectrum of bodies). They questioned the intentions and morals of the attendees. Was the paycheck worth ignoring those on the higher end of the size spectrum who still have the smallest assortment of brands to choose from? In a matter of hours, the conversation grew from heated to inflamed.

What few understood, however, is the behind-the-scenes logistics at play. Because while, yes, only offering up to a size 22 is limited and not for every *body*, the brand in question had major plans to center community—including size expansion—in authentic ways. I know this because I asked. *Before* attending the event, I might add. But because I didn't post that private conversation online, because none of the attendees had, we were met with (to a point) understandable anger.

Many of us wish we could burn capitalism to the ground. It's often regarded as the root of all evil, for justifiable reasons. But the fashion industry is just that: an industry. One so centered in an archaic system grounded in private conversations, favors, and classic butt-kissing that is nearly impossible to escape. It's impossible to determine which form of activism works best against fashion's hierarchy, and what I've come to find is that passionate opinions on that topic vary greatly from advocate to advocate.

Social media has done great things for the plus-size community, allowing many to connect and speak out in ways previously unimaginable. It's also, however, allowed confusion to spread and names to be tarnished and attacked without a sole bit of context to the scandal at hand. In many ways, the digital age has made advocacy feel more performative. Many find it reasonable to push for more transparency from behind closed doors, especially as designers continue to make consumer promises that fall flat time and time again. The unfortunate truth is, however, that that's not how all brands choose to operate.

Before a brand expands their size range, hundreds of conversations are held in private, not to mention limitless hours of work, planning, and construction. To ignore that, to minimize that all by saying "it's easy, just do it," does a disservice to those who put in free labor to help designers truly understand why this customer, this *community*, matters. We are all a part of the system. Understanding that is crucial to determining how, on an individual basis, we can all make change.

The criticism directed toward those who support certain "inclusive" brands is often labeled as anger and jealousy, which falsely categorizes those speaking out. Especially as, more often than not, the ones who do risk their status to publicly advocate for change are Black women on the larger end of the size spectrum, those who are most marginalized within the community. To classify their concerns and frustrations as "anger" minimizes the point at hand. They are not wicked here. Rather, they simply want to be accepted within the conversation, a place they deserve to be heard.

All of us have a voice. All of us have a story, an opinion. And all of us should have the space to express that. Being told your size is unworthy of such is desolating.

Few brands get it right on the first try. In fact, some of the most popular size-inclusive brands today sprouted from messy beginnings. Among them is Target.

In 2014 future cofounder of the CurvyCon Chastity Garner Valentine became increasingly frustrated with Target's fashion offerings. Like many women, the store was her go-to stop and shop for all things home and beauty. But the mere fact that she could knock off all her shopping minus fashion at Target didn't sit right in her style-focused mind. And when the brand announced a major collaboration with Altuzarra, she had simply had enough. A few glasses of wine in, with no concrete intentions other than to express her frustrations, Chastity began typing.

"For so long, I loved you," she wrote. "I always went above and beyond in our relationship. I'll visit you to get a couple of items and more than a couple hundred dollars later and a cart full of products, I have left giving you way more than I ever planned to. No matter how much I give, you never seem to appreciate me. All I want is the clothing you offer all your other regular sized customers, but you always leave me out. With that being said, I have to end this relationship. It's you, not me and for my own well-being and my self dignity I have to sever ties between us."

Chastity continued, "I'm up late, working as usual, and I see Refinery 29 post 50 photos of the newest designer collaboration. Literally 50 pieces of beautiful (and I mean beautiful) affordable clothing and none of it will be remotely close to the size that I wear. The collection consists of deep hues of burgundy, fabulous snakeskin prints, and fall worthy silk-like maxi dresses . . . enough to make any fashion lover lust. My heart sinks. You have once again made me feel like a second-class customer and because of that I'm going to have to discontinue my relationship with you altogether."

Posted to her Facebook page of hundreds of thousands of fans, the letter went unexpectedly viral. Soon enough, her message and voice were everywhere, from social media support to the headlines of major magazines. And when Target reached out personally, Chastity had no idea what was in store. The brand commended Chastity for her honesty, accepting their shortcomings and stating that they wanted to revamp their designs, making them more inclusive to the Target shopper. And because of her boldness, they welcomed Chastity onboard to help oversee and lead the project.

Chastity's letter resembled one written by Marie Denee of *The Curvy Fashionista* a few years prior, in which she wrote, "Why do you ignore, shun, and sweep me to the side when I want to shop too? Each season, you skillfully and beautifully execute exclusive designer collaborations and partnerships with the leading fashion designers—all to make high fashion attainable to the American woman—yet you ignore me. As plus size women, we are often neglected, overlooked and always sized out of your collections."

The reaction to Chastity's Target takeover was mixed, however. While met with much support from the plus-size community, some felt that we shouldn't have to convince brands to cater to us. If they don't want our money, why get on our knees and beg for scraps? On the other hand, however, is accessibility. At the time, clothing options for bigger women were still scarce. With Target's soon-to-be expansion into plus, a curvy shopper could get the well-fitting suit she needed for a job interview for well under a hundred dollars.

It's a two-sided coin, a conundrum with no universally accepted answer. When it comes to straight-size fashion, it is the job of a brand to market to the customer. The brand must, in whatever ways possible, convince customers that its clothes are worth the hard-earned money sitting in their bank accounts. It is the brand's job to put in the work. When it comes to extended sizes, however, everything is reversed. Despite plus-size women making up the majority of American shoppers, brands expect the consumers to convince them, time and time again, of their worth. The statistic that over 68 percent of American women are plus size isn't enough. Without loud noise to show designers without a doubt that if they expand, revenue will increase, taking the plunge into plus is near impossible.

But why must the effort—both physical and emotional—always be placed on the women who, until recently, have been told their voice doesn't matter? When will big brands begin to truly cater to plus, and not just begrudgingly meet undeniably lucrative demands?

"You have to appeal to this customer on an emotional basis," Chastity says. "Something that makes them feel good, that makes them feel included. There's so many parameters around being a plus-size shopper, and if you can't get that quite right, you can get roasted, and we've seen that many times before."

The success of Target set an industry-wide precedent for how to nail plus sizes: by centering community every step of the way. Other brands have built on this strategy over the years with standout collaborations that set a proven track record for those hoping to dive into extended sizes, like Priscilla Ono x Eloquii, Gabifresh x Swimsuits For All, Isabel Toledo x Lane Bryant, and Rihanna's Savage X Fenty.

Another brand to make a splash: Old Navy. In August 2021 seven years after receiving backlash for charging more for plus sizes and not carrying them in store, the brand reemerged with a new dedication: Bod-Equality. Years in the making, Old Navy announced that sizes up to a 28 would now be stocked in its over 1,200 stores internationally. Prices would remain the same across sizes, and every style would be sold in every size. Diverse mannequins were to be placed in each store, and the company's website was to be reconstructed to do away with the plus-size-specific sections for women.

Old Navy's move was largely celebrated by the community at large who finally felt like they were heard, even if it took many years to happen. There were missteps and rooms for improvement, however; the retailer announced that their biggest size—a size 30—would only be sold online, making customers question why such a measure needed to be taken for only one size. Why not include all in stores if it's just one extra size? Yet despite that, Old Navy's move made it the first major retailer to accomplish such a big feat. And in that, proved that it is both possible and financially sustainable for major brands to follow suit.

The key to nailing plus is simple: care about the customer. A huge proponent of that message is Nadia Aboulhosn, a Middle Eastern blogger turned model, designer, and multihyphenate.

"It's really exciting to see the community really pushing [for true inclusivity] because they wanted to see it, regardless of if brands were on the same page as them at the time," Nadia says. "The community needed to see it."

As we chat, Nadia reminisces on the early days, when as a baby blogger, she'd respond to direct messages from brands by trying her best to convince them to expand sizes. No opportunity was too little for change. And no brand, no matter how big, could silence her voice. Now, years later, she's perhaps most well known for her frequent collaborations with Fashion to Figure, particularly in regard to her iconic thigh-high boots.

Behind the scenes, Nadia, as she puts it, "ruined" multiple relationships with brands that found her demands—the demands of our community—to be too much, too bold, too loud. It took years to find teams who would not only listen but also care enough to act on what Nadia knew this customer so direly craved. All of that work was worth it in the end.

Ariana Grande–esque but make it curvy, Nadia's boot collaboration with FTF was a long time coming. Before connecting with the brand, she spent the years since 2013 trying to convince everyone and anyone that what plus-size women needed more than anything were some sexy boots. After all, what's more powerful than stomping into your purpose in boots that not only fit flawlessly but also perfectly capture the badass you are?

"[What I told them was] what I want is thigh-high boots," Nadia recalls, "and they were like, 'Okay. No questions.' I was completely shocked. Love to see it!"

Multiple iterations in, Nadia's boots have evolved season after season to become the go-to destination for big-girl calves. And to think, if only a brand had listened to her and her community-driven voice back in 2013, perhaps it would have come sooner. But it took FTF to break the chain and listen in a true, meaningful way.

It shouldn't be a surprise that FTF has become a changemaker in the space. Nick Kaplan, the company's current president, is the great grandson of Lena Bryant. Yes, *that* Lena Bryant, the one who launched Lane Bryant a century ago and who ignited the spark for change throughout this industry. You could say inclusivity runs through Nick's blood, and it shows, both in the ways he runs the brand and the manner in which he passionately speaks about it.

Nick launched FTF back in 2004 alongside his brother, Michael, naming it in honor of their great-grandmother who famously said, "Never ask women to conform their figures to fashion, but rather bring fashion to the figure." While their father ran Lane Bryant during their adolescence, the company sold before the two were old enough to have a part in its success. Even still, Nick recalls traveling to the New York City offices with his father, loading up the cups of hot chocolate on the weekends and heading into stores. "I just remember being *part* of it, and seeing what it really was," Nick says.

In college the two brothers went separate ways, Nick down a more entrepreneurial road and Michael on an Ivy League path. But postgraduation they came together to see how they could incorporate their skills and wealth of knowledge into a company that would not only make a change but also serve those size 24 gals who could never find clothes at their local mall. That's how FTF was born. Launching with a three-thousand-square-foot storefront on the first floor of the Palisades Center mall in West Nyack, New York, a new revolution had begun.

"Our thesis was that not all women want to shop in the store that treats them as a second-class citizen," Nick says. "This is a segment of the population that's growing, and not just growing in terms of the number of people but growing in their confidence and their wanting more."

FTF has built a community from the inside out over the years, surrounding itself with people who truly get it—particularly with their influencer partners—and who know this customer on the most personal level. Because it is that feeling of togetherness—behind the scenes and through the brand's digital presence—that has moved many to support and trust them through the changing tides.

"We can't be transactional," he explains. "It isn't about revenue. It's about customer connection. If you build it, they will come, which is sort of corny but true. You have to have that level of confidence and belief in what you're doing, and that group of people around you who get it, that can help execute it."

In their expansion and evolution, FTF has served this customer by refining their voice and understanding that this community is not a monolith that can be served equally. Rather, they have a specific style, one very different from Ashley Stewart or Lane Bryant or Target or Old Navy. For the customers who want to feel sexy, empowered, and as bold as can be, FTF is their go-to destination. And for those who don't, there's no bad blood. Because as Nick witnessed in that Palisades mall back in 2004, women sizes 2, 4, 6, and 8 had not only a plethora of options available to them but also the widest spectrum of styles and aesthetics. Curvy girls deserve the same, and with FTF they hope to tackle one crucial part of the market.

What perhaps FTF has done best in recent years is put their money and support behind influencers and models of color in the community who are often not granted major collaboration opportunities from "traditional" fashion brands. In addition to

Nadia, the brand has frequently collaborated with Chastity, Tabria Majors, La'Tecia Thomas, and Patrick Starrr, among others.

The power of community is vastly underrated, despite the years of evidence showing how it is, in fact, the key to success in the plus-size space. The issue has become evident with brands like LOFT that, after less than two years of expanding sizes, shuttered plus in the midst of the pandemic to cut costs. It was a moment that enraged many, myself included. Having had many intriguing conversations with the brand over the months pre-COVID, it blew my mind to see them abandon plus so easily. But, when analyzing the situation, it suddenly all made sense: they had never made a true commitment to this community.

Despite making loads of noise to celebrate their launch, LOFT never stocked plus sizes in store. Online, their extended-size offering was laughable compared to that of our thin counterparts. Their marketing only reflected a very limited version of plus. It should have been no surprise, then, that our voices were never truly reflected behind the scenes.

One would think that in the midst of a pandemic where money is tight, leaning into plus sizes, which make up 68 percent of American women, would be key to staying afloat. But this customer, this community, is too smart to fall for half-assed tricks. Devotion, trust, and authenticity must be centered for success to come. Differences and divides in the plus-size community may make it seem like everyone is on a different path, their hopes set on different missions and methods to get there. But ask any fat fashionista why they do what they do, and their answers will all align: they do it for each other. They do it for their younger selves. They do it for the next generation. But most of all, they do it for the community. Because without that behind them, nothing is possible.

6

RUNWAYS AND REDEMPTION

I COULDN'T HAVE FELT more like Miranda Priestly at my first fashion week.

You'd think—from the way I was dressed, my manner of grooming, the antisocial and slightly terrified look plastered across my face—I was more like Andy Sachs, pretransformation (perhaps even worse, to be honest, considering my Walmart jeans were practically sprayed on). But none of that mattered. Because as I entered the studio that day, I could hear Miranda's infamous words filling my every brain cell: "Everybody wants this. Everyone wants to be us."

I realized quickly, however, that *I* was not the one everyone aspired to be. I was the *other*.

In the summer of 2018 I made the move from my hometown in Upstate New York to Manhattan, interning at a digital entertainment company. It was a fine gig. My coworkers were perhaps some of the funniest individuals I've had the pleasure of working beside. But as the days went on, I felt myself drawn further and further from the world of entertainment and its daily gossip spirals. What I really wanted, more than anything, was to maneuver myself from our midtown office to the stylish streets of Soho, where fashion reigned, and social status was a prerequisite for entry.

I spent that summer commuting between midtown and the World Trade Center, home of the illustrious Condé Nast offices, networking with any editor who would give me the time of day. I'd often leave for my hour-long allotted lunch break and return two hours later, filled with knowledge and inspiration, not a thought in my mind that my then boss would become aggravated by my prolonged absence. We made jokes about it as the summer went on. But really, I was the worst employee.

Nevertheless, midway through that summer, I launched a fashion blog, as all young hopefuls seemed to do, called *Hard At #Werk*, a destination to explore plus-size menswear like never before. A few days later I crafted a Twitter rant about the lack of clothing options available to a young man like myself. And by chance, it came across the newsfeed of the then editor in chief of *NYLON*, Gabrielle Korn. It only took her a few days to reach out via email, asking if I'd like to cover the topic at New York Fashion Week: Men's later that month.

Suddenly, by way of 180 Twitter characters, I went from intern to fashion reporter, traveling into the depths of Soho for my first fashion week. Seated front row, it all seemed like a fantasy, one fueled by the youthful excitement that filled my veins. As we waited for the show to begin—fashion shows almost religiously start thirty minutes late—I waited for the other shoe to drop: Would I be kicked out of my seat to make room for someone more important? Would my presence be questioned by an ill-spirited PR person? Would I pass out under the heat and nerves of it all?

It all went perfectly.

What I did notice, quite quickly, was that despite my inner confidence (and ego, if we're being honest) in that moment, I was the *only* fat person in the room. I was the anomaly, the rare occurrence, the *other*. And I'd soon realize, in the months and years to come, that that would often be the case.

There's power in being the first to win, to succeed, to break down barriers. But it often feels so bittersweet to do so alone.

Fashion week is notorious for being the epicenter of elitist attitudes and condescending glares. It is everything movies like *The Devil Wears Prada* make it out to be, sometimes kinder in certain circles, and often worse for those who push the boundaries on what the industry deems acceptable. That includes plus-size folk.

Despite progress in the retail and mass-market space, fashion week has, until recently, remained resistant to change in regard to size inclusivity. Whereas the Targets of the world have begun to understand the value in curvy shoppers, not all luxury designers are convinced that plus sells. Do fat women really want high-end dresses? Can they afford flawlessly tailored pantsuits? Are they even confident enough to wear them? All of these questions I've heard in conversations with designers over the years.

Fashion week—and Fashion Month as a whole, which comprises runways in New York, Milan, London, and Paris—sets the tone for the seasons to come, not just in trends but in inclusivity. As diversity becomes increasingly incorporated into the collections and inspirations for designers, the question of "What are you doing to prioritize marginalized voices within the scope of your brand?" has become crucial.

Progress has been made, sometimes in large ways, others in small but powerful steps. According to the Fashion Spot's seasonal diversity report in September 2019, sixty-eight plus-size models were used during New York Fashion Week. That number dwindled in the seasons to follow, likely influenced by the pandemic's impact on the industry, with only twelve used in September 2020. But the exact number matters perhaps less than the brands that decide to take the plunge.

Before the pandemic the use of plus-size models was almost entirely dependent on a few key designers who have clung to plus in recent years, like Christian Siriano, Tanya Taylor, Tadashi Shoji, Chromat, and Tommy Hilfiger. But most recently, legendary brands that have never stepped foot into plus have broken barriers in the most exciting ways.

In September 2020 Versace cast three plus-size models—Paloma Elsesser, Alva Claire, and Jill Kortleve—to walk in its Milan Fashion Week show, a historic feat for the brand. Just a few months earlier, Paloma and Jill also became the first two curve girls to walk in a Fendi show. That same season, Chanel sent Jill down the catwalk in Paris, their first time using a curve model in a decade. And in mid-2021 Jacquemus took the plunge by casting Yumi Nu, a rising star for the plus community, in its summer show.

These wins, although more isolated, push the boundaries in enormous ways. Because if Donatella Versace thinks curves are cool, who's to say otherwise?

Maybe one of the most iconic fashion week moments to occur in the past decade was at the hands of 11 Honoré, a digital shopping destination aimed at creating a simplified way for luxury fashion brands—like Prabal Gurung, Brandon Maxwell, Marchesa, Zac Posen, and Michael Kors—to enter the plus-size space. Forming numerous popular designer collaborations since its launch in 2017, the platform has brought luxury and size diversity together in a groundbreaking way. And in 2019 that message hit the runway of fashion week with one of the most breathtaking shows to date.

"It was a totally different side of fashion week that we don't always get to see," says Lauren Alexis Fisher, former digital fashion editor at *Harper's BAZAAR*. "It was just about celebrating the joy of fashion and the beauty of inclusivity. . . It's one of those pinch-me fashion week moments where you're like, 'Okay, this is why I'm doing it. This is why I'm in this industry.'"

Lauren remembers that night perfectly, recalling it as being her ultimate fashion week standout moment of the season. Because while most shows and events can feel draining, 11 Honoré's runway debut was electrifying. Gathering together the industry's top curve models, the show featured a wide range of women sizes 10 and above in the most elegant of gowns, a truly unforeseen sight for decades prior. And to close the show was none other than Laverne Cox, styled to perfection in a bright pink gown, sewn together with hundreds of layers of pink and red tulle. As she sashayed and twirled down the runway, confetti bursting from the ceiling above, and a herd of gorgeous plus-size gals behind her, everyone in the audience could feel it: *this* is fashion, baby.

"That is the fashion week content people are moved and inspired by, moments where it feels like everybody is being celebrated and everybody has a place," Lauren says. "That show, that moment, that finale really brought back that spark that initially drew me to the fashion industry. . . . It was representing the shift in fashion, and the future of where it was going rather than the buttoned-up, super-boring, straight-laced show that is just for one person and one small sector of the world."

This is fashion. This is why we fight, why we beg for change. Because we know—*we know*—just how much these clothes, these moments, and these women have the power to change our entire lives. I can't say it enough: plus-size fashion is transformative. For some, it's lifesaving. It's the encouragement we need in our darkest moments, the strength to lift us from the deepest pits of personal hell and agony. All of this—all of *us*—is about so much more than clothes. It's about being granted the permission to live, to breathe, and to thrive in our most natural, raw states. It's about rising above the hate, the turmoil to speak boldly and proudly of the things that make us different, the things that make us most beautiful. We bring plus-size fashion to life because we are the stories fueling its core.

Moments like that—often unimaginable—are what excite me most. A few seasons into my fashion career, I made the concentrated decision to stop attending noninclusive runway shows altogether. That choice was largely driven by Hunter McGrady, who made a similar commitment in 2019. Seeing her devotion to inclusivity—not solely of size, but of *all*—regardless of the financial losses that came with it was the example I needed to follow.

The fact of the matter is, designers who don't dress diverse body types bore me. It's as simple as that. And yes, perhaps their designs are lovely, beautifully crafted and inspired. But runway shows that don't reflect the world at large—*my* world—lack the emotional resonance I desperately crave. There's nothing like the excitement that comes when a stunning plus-size model struts the runway, commanding attention and beauty and elegance. Now *that's* fashion. Anything else is—while perhaps remarkable to some—not for me.

"We're still growing in the realm of fashion week in terms of size inclusion," says model-turned-editor-turned-designer-turned-ultimate-multihyphenate Lauren Chan. "I can't wait to see some plus-size bodies on the runway for couture. I certainly hope that it happens because I feel like that would be the next appropriate step. But we're also growing in the way that not only one person is walking super luxury designer shows, but a handful are. And to me, that's a huge feat considering just a few years ago, it seemed as if there was only one model doing that."

What excites Lauren most about the future is seeing the emphasis around size inclusivity be normalized in New York and spread deeper into the more prestigious European markets. The tally on how many curve girls were used may vary, but the impact of seeing a historic Versace moment is undeniable.

"In 2017 [the plus-size] models were all in New York Fashion Week shows," she explains. "And now they're happening in

Paris, which if you're a fan of fashion, you know is the epicenter of fashion, and the trickle-down effect from Paris is paramount. And also, they're the least inclusive. So it's a different KPI; it's a different point of success to compare. And I'm really excited by this new development and this new form of growth."

This paradigm shift has also moved to put straight and plus sizes on the same level playing field. In the traditional fashion world, designers would jump on the chance to cast a fresh face, a groundbreaking talent that only they had the exclusive to introduce. For years, however, plus sizes operated oppositely. Models like Ashley Graham were required to cement their talent and celebrity status before being welcomed onto runways. Finally, that's begun to change. With plus becoming the prize to win, legendary fashion houses are realizing the potential that comes with introducing the next Queen of Curves.

"To use the KPI of 'Do we want to be treated equally to straight size models?' if we're using that as a measure of success, then I think that we've made great strides just this past season alone."

Lauren began her career as a journalist, blazing her way through Condé Nast's hallowed halls as *Glamour's* fashion editor extraordinaire. It was there that she not only helped to expand the mainstream conversation around size inclusivity but also had the opportunity to work on the design side of the magazine's collaboration with Lane Bryant. All of it would build toward launching her own luxury brand, Henning, designed and fabricated specifically for the working woman.

"At that time, we had representation, we were starting to see models break into the mainstream and become properly famous, we had content, and yet we were still having a hard time getting dressed," she says. "I was missing clothes to wear to the office that made me feel as commanding as my peers, that made me look as capable, specifically because I worked in fashion. So what you wear really matters."

What Lauren quickly realized, however, is that while her everyday experience would help catapult Henning into existence, finding her customer would be a battle all its own. Because while the Fashion Novas of the world have made curvy women reconnect with their sexy side, the luxury plus-size shopper is one who, until recently, has only been discussed in theory.

To dive deep in finding those who, like Lauren, desperately craved womenswear that fit and felt fabulous, she launched Henning's digital platform six months early, centering community in each step of the process through the brand's Instagram channel, email program, and private Facebook group "in order to ask women what they were missing, what kind of features they wanted, if they prefer covered buttons or horn buttons, etc."

It only took a mere matter of months for that extra labor and outreach to pay off. Two years into Henning, the brand has been featured in nearly every major media outlet while being worn by trailblazers like Stacey Abrams and Ashley Graham.

"When I'm having a tough day at work and I need a little bit of extra grit to get through some troubleshooting, or I need inspiration on what to design next, I go through customer reviews and emails, or I go on Instagram, and I interact with customers in DMs. Because that's the best possible way to gauge a reaction."

Lauren adds, "Plus-size women are multifaceted people. I have customers that are film directors, that are lawyers, that are mainstream politicians, that are award-winning journalists, that are famous models. When people like that have been relegated to shopping clothing meant for teenagers, there's a celebration that happens when they find a brand like Henning, because I hope that they finally feel seen, finally feel like their self-worth is being reflected back to them, and that they aren't just an afterthought."

The reason for why the luxury world has only recently adventured into inclusive sizing is simple: money. Capitalism reigns supreme, after all, particularly in this subset of the industry that is kept alive by higher price points and designer names that often hold more value than the very garments themselves. But beneath the excuse "Well, plus sizes just don't make financial sense for us" lies a handful of more truthful answers to why designers stray from curves. Some fear they can't execute it properly, having never designed for plus before. Others are so far out of touch with this customer that it's hard to fathom understanding their desires. And many are simply too fatphobic to care.

With data and a proven track record, any level-headed designer would take the time to learn how extended sizes may boost their bottom line. And that's precisely why Lauren and Henning are so crucial to the industry: Because the brand's very existence sets a powerful precedent for others to follow. And when lumped alongside forward-thinking designers like Christian Siriano, well, we become all the more unstoppable.

Christian is a fashion legend for far more than just his inventive and stunning gowns. He is the very definition of how to be a leader rather than follower, a surefire success story of how to turn outdated tropes on their heads, creating wonderful, inclusive art along the way. Ask any New York fashionista from within the plus-size community, and they'll likely be able to regale you with a story of Christian filling their heart with joy. If their stories are anything like mine, it'll be a clear example of why inclusivity matters so deeply.

My very first exposure to fashion came back in 2007 when, at age ten, I witnessed Christian win season four of *Project Runway*. It was a moment that resonated with me so profoundly, though I wouldn't be able to fully understand why until more than a decade later. His determination, grit, passion, and exuberance told my chubby elementary school self that there was a place in the world for someone like me: someone who was different, who was bold, and who craved the space to express it freely.

Christian's influence on my life was immediate. I'd spend hours each week creating garments for my stuffed animals out of cut-up socks, shirts, and scraps I could find. In fifth grade a dear friend by the name of Jo Ann assisted me in organizing a wedding for my most prized and beloved Webkinz—a pug named Muffin—in which I constructed a dress made entirely out of toilet paper. I felt revolutionary.

My sewing skills took a backseat as I began to dive into the world of musical theater soon after. Yet when fashion reentered my life in college, I quickly reconnected with my adoration of Christian and his successes, which had only grown larger and better in the decade since his *Project Runway* win.

I met Christian for the first time at a fashion event in New Jersey, which I aggressively forced a friend to drive me to only a few hours prior with my heart set on making the connection come to life. In the coming years, I'd interview him on several occasions, my nerves and excitement rising each time. But in February of 2020 I'd attend my first Christian Siriano runway show. And it changed my life.

Preshow, I ventured backstage to interview Marquita Pring, a fashion week and industry game changer whose fierceness is difficult to describe in few words. The backstage scene was just like I'd been told: a bewildering, hot (and fabulous) mess. With hardly enough room to squeeze my plump body through the hair and makeup stations, I sat and marveled at the fact that in just a decade, I'd gone from crafting "designer" toilet paper gowns to breathing the same air as the very person who inspired me to do so.

The show that evening was everything: glitz, glam, power, beauty. Christian's shows are more than just fashion; they're a celebration. A celebration of life, of imagination, of *inclusivity.* Few moments feel as "pinch-me" worthy as that one.

"That energy is in the air at his shows," Lauren explains, having walked her first Christian Siriano runway midpandemic. "Show day is always really exciting because when you get there, it's everything we always saw in the movies or pictured in our minds. It's an exciting emotional moment because it feels like a breakthrough on true inclusion."

She adds, "It's transformative and it's emotional, and if you really think about it, it's the kids who were always left out finally being allowed at the party."

Christian credits his passion for inclusivity to his household growing up. "My sister wanted to look one way, my mother wanted to look another, and that was very inspiring," he tells me. His sister—who studied ballet—was a size 0 and his mother a size 16, that spectrum always present in the young designer's eyes. Attending high school in Baltimore City furthered that: "It was a totally different world, but I loved it. I really wanted to embrace it."

Diversity was always the norm to young Christian, and has remained so in the decades since. His theory is simple—if you want a fabulous dress, you should get a fabulous dress, no matter your size, age, race, or gender. Fashion, like beauty, is in the eye of the beholder and should be accessible to everyone, regardless of status or wealth.

While heavily known for his jaw-dropping runways, since his brand's inception, Christian has put the same amount of design effort and detail into clothing of all price points. Because there is no one singular Siriano girl. All who want to wear his designs should have the ability to do so.

That notably took form in his collaborations with Payless and Lane Bryant. It was an interesting space to navigate for the new designer, particularly as he entered the industry around the time of the 2008 market crash when many brands went under. Rather than limit his potential reach to thousands of women, his affordable collaborations introduced his name to millions.

After working with Ashley Graham, Candice Huffine, and other soon-to-be-legendary models for a Lane Bryant campaign, Christian began to question why these extraordinary women weren't attending his fashion week castings. The opportunity had simply never been presented to them before, but Christian intentionally changed that, requesting them specifically to come and walk and be welcomed in a new space. Any one of his models will tell you that few rooms are as welcoming as a Christian Siriano spectacle.

As Christian describes it, "The energy at our shows is always so special—which is why I still love doing them—because I don't fill the room with close-minded people. I don't fill the backstage with the same models, they're all different. Clothes should make us feel good. That is so important to remember."

Christian's dedication to size inclusivity works so well because his inspiration is driven not from trends but from the very people he dresses. From his red-carpet celebrities to inner-circle friends, surrounding himself with a diverse room of widely different perspectives has been key to understanding why it matters to make fashion for all.

"Our biggest customers are all curvy, size 12, 14, and 16. Those are our biggest clients. Even our brides now, we have brides in every size. We had a bride who was a size 28/30. She was a very voluptuous woman, and then we had a bride who was literally a 00. We have it all, and I love that."

He adds, "What we do is not supposed to be this hard, difficult thing. It's supposed to be fun, so that's really the goal. Always was. . . . My goal is to just make every type of inclusion, in whatever we're doing, just part of the business every day. There is no conversation anymore about it, we don't even think about it that way. It has to just be. You have to normalize it."

And when it comes to his advice for the next generation of trailblazing designers, Christian is clear:

> There really are no rules. It never used to be that way. You really used to have to go through every hurdle and hoop to build a business and find a customer. But now, it's really about connecting with the people you want to sell to, who you want to build with. It's not enough to just make cool clothes. You have to have more than that, and I think those are the young designers who will be most successful.

Christian has helped set a precedent at fashion week for the importance of including curve models. But he's certainly not alone. Perhaps the most inclusive and all-welcoming is Chromat, which is equal parts fashion and party, wrapped into the most thrilling experience you'll find in New York's fashion district.

Creating "future-forward" swim and bodywear, Chromat's core is centered on feeling your most powerful, even when wearing the least. And its founder, Becca McCharen-Tran, is the ultimate changemaker many of us one day aspire to be, myself included. What began as an after-work art project confined to the walls of her small-town Virginia apartment would, over the course of a few years, become one of the most revolutionary brands to grace the runways of New York Fashion Week.

An architect major turned drama-club costumer, Becca's vision behind Chromat was to create "scaffolding for the body." Raiding the bridal section of Jo Ann Fabrics for corsetry supplies, her artistic and innovative eye found inspiration in the most unlikely of places. She began by designing for her closest friends, all of whom were of different shapes and sizes, ingraining inclusivity into the very foundation of Chromat. Then, a few years later, an architect colleague would introduce Becca to his daughter, who would soon ask her to be part of a pop-up shop on the Lower East Side. The outcome? Chromat was an instant hit. And in 2014 the brand's legacy was cemented when curvy supermodel Denise Bidot opened up their fall runway show.

Becca recalls that moment—in which Denise donned an iconic Chromat cage piece—as shocking for the industry, busting through a then-untouched barrier on who the faces of fashion week could include. But even more important, it served as the most beautiful moment of personal healing.

"As a girl growing up, looking at magazines and absorbing the media imagery, I struggled a lot with an eating disorder," Becca recalls. "And I was really turned off by the fashion industry once I went into recovery from that, because for me growing up, I thought being fashionable meant being skinny and being able to afford all the clothes at the mall. . . . So I knew that whatever I did in this creative space, I wanted to make sure that there was intention to highlight different types of people who have been excluded from fashion."

What's propelled Chromat to excel in the hectic fashion week landscape is the brand's dedication to inclusivity. Not just of one or two, but of *all* people. The conversation around diversity at fashion week can often begin to feel like an overly simplified checklist. Many will call it a day after casting one curve girl and another model of color, meeting their "diversity quota" for the season. But that is the definition of performative activism. Chromat has embraced inclusivity for its true meaning. Beyond casting models of size, Becca and her team are intent on including Black models, models of color, trans and nonbinary models, disabled models, and anyone else who has been marginalized and punished by this industry for their sheer existence. She credits much of this all-embracing message to her lived experience as a queer and mid-/plus-size person living in New York City. Surrounding herself with the very communities she aims to represent has been fundamental to Chromat's extraordinary evolution. And it's a surefire example for others to follow.

"When I've heard feedback from people saying, 'This was the first time I saw someone that looked like me, or saw someone walking that was plus size, or saw someone with crutches,' I know how powerful that feeling is, because I felt it too. It switches something in your brain where you're like, 'Oh, wait, that could be me. That means that I'm special. That means that I'm desirable. That means that I'm worthy.'"

To a point, designers like Becca and Christian make it seem easy. If they can perfectly construct sizes for a wide spectrum of bodies, why can't others? A report from *InStyle* published in February 2020 found that only 22 percent of designers that showed at New York Fashion Week produced a size 20 or above. A major reason for that? Many simply don't know where to start.

Fashion education is perhaps doing one of the largest disservices to the next generation of designers as an overwhelming majority of top institutions have yet to implement plus-size-specific training into their curriculum. I was shocked and taken back when reporting on this topic for Refinery29 in early 2020, but it all suddenly made sense. If designers—particularly those who are not plus size themselves and lack an understanding of that lived experience—aren't shown that plus is possible and within reach, then how are they to believe it is vital to the future of their success?

I spent the early months of 2020 contacting, interviewing, and tracking down the industry's top educators to ask them, plainly and simply, why plus was not yet a priority at their schools. I was met with promises and pledges, most of which—if not all—have not been met over a year later. They may blame the pandemic for halting their "plans" to expand into inclusive fashion education, but wouldn't a global shift on what the future of fashion is only encourage one to emphasize the importance of size diversity? Perhaps that's too much to ask from those who have never been rejected by this industry themselves.

At a majority of fashion schools, plus is an elective afterthought. Students can, if they so wish, focus on designing for diverse bodies in their senior projects, though the resources they'll be given to do so are limited. The most frustrating part, however, is that these students are begging for it, more so than ever before. Nearly every educator I've spoken with has agreed: gen Z craves inclusivity.

Much of the work that's been done to implement inclusive fashion education has been accomplished by curve industry leaders themselves, those who understand firsthand how important it is not only to give students the opportunity to learn but also to show them how critical curves are to the future of this world. Among these fighters is supermodel Emme, who launched Fashion Without Limits in 2013, an initiative cofounded with Syracuse University's School of Design professors Jeffrey Mayer and Todd Conover. With her is Susan Moses, a famed celebrity stylist and author of the book *The Art of Dressing Curves: The Best-Kept Secrets of a Fashion Stylist*.

Susan served as executive producer of FIT's "The Business of Curves," a forum first held in 2017 that also included associate producers Emme and Catherine Schuller. Moderated by Fern Mallis, creator of New York Fashion Week, the conversation focused on the rapid growth and expansion of plus sizes in recent years. The event was so popular among students, in fact, that it moved the school's faculty to implement curve design into various technical courses. It was clear: students understand how important plus sizes are. It is time educators step up to help.

"The forum was filled to capacity, we had great press coverage and garnered the cover of the business section of WWD," Susan recalls. "There was substantial engagement with the students in the weeks following the event and led to connecting students with internships with curvy brands through the director of internships at FIT. . . . The lack of plus-size education has resulted in years of a problematic fit in the plus-size clothing industry because technical design isn't being considered for plus-size specifications. Plus-size is not being discussed or taught from a stylistic point of view, and fashion is still being taught and revered from a thin perspective. It's really time the schools help break the myth that fashion stops at a size 10. Students have been ready to embrace curves for a long time. Schools need to join them."

She adds, "After engaging with several schools regarding the plus curriculum, I believe that some of [their hesitation] is prejudice. But the majority is bureaucracy and the fear of changing the narrative around who is fashionable, who deserves fashion, and the values that have been placed on being thin and fashionable. We must continue to have quality dialogue around this topic in the plus community and with the fashion institutions. The latter is really key."

Ben Barry, dean of fashion at Parsons School of Design, is also a huge proponent of change. "Students are excited, ready and have a significant desire to design for all bodies," he says. "They want to work in an industry that is inclusive, that does center plus-size bodies in very real, legitimate, and valuable ways."

At fourteen Ben launched a modeling agency from the comfort of his family's basement. It all stemmed from seeing a close friend—who was a size 16/18—being told she was too big to be signed to a pre-existing agency. "I knew nothing about fashion, but I wanted to help," he explains. Angered, he sent her photos to a local magazine that, interested in publishing them, assumed Ben was her agent. Within fifteen years, the Ben Barry Agency went on to represent over 150 models. All of it laid the foundation for the work he was set to accomplish.

"There was a gap in the market, but I think even deeper than that, there was really systemic exclusion when we thought about plus-size bodies in fashion, and realizing that was one way to change that. . . . Models are critical, but to really make the deep change that is needed, we need to change the world views of the next generation of decision makers and designers. And that's what inspired me to move into education."

Ben notes that an inclusive fashion education draws on the already-existing work of fat activists who have simply never been invited into these elite industry spaces. The knowledge exists; it's simply a matter of giving it space to be transmitted to the next generation.

"I hope fashion education continues to really honor and respect and draw on the work of fat studies and the work of fat activists to develop a set of world views that then inspire practices for fashion education. Part of that is ensuring that there are specific hiring faculty members who are trained in these areas, faculty members who have experience in fat studies and fat activism."

He adds, "When we think about fatphobia and the thin ideal in fashion education and the fashion industry at large, that is a direct result of colonization of the transatlantic slave trade and, of course, White supremacy. And so, part of a push for an inclusive fashion curriculum is centering Black feminist thought and centering intersectionality. And so, what that means is in very deliberate, intentional ways, disrupting how fashion teaches about gender, how fashion teaches about race, how fashion teaches about disability, and how fashion teaches about fat and plus-size bodies."

Designers like Tanya Taylor—whose contemporary clothing and swimwear is available in sizes 0 through 22—are adamant about inclusive fashion education, as they've seen firsthand how challenging plus can be without the tools and knowledge to nail fit on the first try.

What Tanya's found over the years is that there's an educational divide between brands and customers, especially when it comes to price point. Only recently has luxury and contemporary clothing—like Tanya Taylor's vibrant, joyful designs—been available in extended sizes as for years, the only options for a size 18 shopper were fast fashion and mass-market picks. Convincing and explaining why a $450 sundress is worth the investment took time and, more specifically, loads of conversation directly with leading community members who could, in turn, relay the message to their audiences. And now, years into their size expansion, Tanya explains that all that extra work to connect with this customer was well worth the investment: "We've noticed that when we launch a new collection, our sales are hugely driven at full price by extended-sized customers. There is no price resistance now, and I think it was just us having to introduce ourselves to that market and build that trust."

Many designers will fit their clothing on a size 4, then grade up—meaning add an extra inch or so per size—without fitting on any additional body types. This practice fails to recognize the variations in size as more weight is added to the body. "They're really missing the shape nuances that change as a body changes," Tanya explains. Rather, fitting on a range of bodies (or at minimum, at least one straight-size model and one plus) allows a designer to more accurately serve all customers, making both their job and her life easier.

Danielle Williams-Eke, 11 Honoré's in-house design director, adds, "Women carry their weight differently, so you have to adjust the pattern differently. When we were kind of going through our design and fit process, we did a full size run and tried it on women sizes 12 to 26 to get their feedback on fit."

She continues, "If you want to be inclusive and go up to 24, 26, and so on and so forth, it can't just be the same pattern, the same fit model, sometimes not even the same pattern maker, because they don't understand the plus-size body in the same way."

Having the chance to speak directly with curvy models allows you to understand the simple, yet profound, design decisions that need to be made to accommodate larger bodies, like straps that are wide enough to cover broader bras, support and comfort through the bust area, and adjustability and stretch for the whole body. Fit models and extensive research are expensive, however, and the process requires a dedication of both resources and time. But as Tanya, Danielle, and many other designers will tell you, it is always worth it.

"She loves fashion as much as anyone," Tanya says. "She looks good in fashion as much as anyone. And why would that be different? This customer absolutely has no difference in how they want to play with fashion than a standard size 4 customer. It's just a different body type. And I think that same kind of zest for playful fashion exists, and we've proven it has. I love that what we've learned over the past few years of having extended sizing is the similarities and not the differences."

That, perhaps, is the most important takeaway. What plus-size women want more than anything is not more, not other. It's *equal*.

Fashion week itself is a broken model. How can an event grounded in the very pursuit of exclusivity suddenly pivot to a message of equality? Dismantling that system as a whole may be impossible without abolishing it and starting from scratch. What we can do, however, is use our individual voices, platforms, and stories to infiltrate the industry and show the importance and vitality of curves, even if it means only gaining one designer on board each season. The fight is slow, but the potential is unimaginable.

That thought is always front of mind anytime I attend fashion week. I'm reminded that my very presence in those spaces as a visibly fat person is a leap of progress all on its own. We often focus our attention on the models and designers, but where fashion continuously lacks is reflecting that inclusivity within the seats at each runway. It's why Chromat shows are so beautiful; not only can you absorb stunning art but you also are able to do so while surrounded by the most beautifully diverse, curated group of attendees. It's an indescribable feeling of welcomeness that is rare, even for the most popular of plus-size industry folk.

Like many, I've had my fair share of terrifying fashion week experiences. Like one show, when a (note: thin) PR person attempted to give my front-row seat to that of another editor, without a concern in the world of where I would be placed instead. Whereas usually I become timid and silenced in those moments, something came over me—I believe it to be the Gucci fanny pack I was wearing at the time, which gave me a certain sense of uncharacteristic entitlement—as I muttered the words, "Actually, I was sitting there." The shock on the PR person's face was enough to remind me of how rare speaking out is in an industry that thrives on the silence of marginalized folk.

Or the time when, weeks before the start of the pandemic, I was denied access to a handful of shows simply because my title of "freelance fashion writer" was not prestigious enough. It didn't matter that I had planned to cover the shows, or that I had a proven track record of reporting on these specific designers. Not enough prestige to my name meant no entry. The gag came when I showed up that evening, using my editor's front row ticket in her place. We fat folk always find a way. Still, it was enough to have me tearing up in a midtown Chick-fil-A later that evening (unfortunately, I am not exaggerating here). Enough to almost make me forgo fashion week altogether, because if I'm not wanted, then why should I even attend?

The fight can start to feel like an unbearable weight in those moments. Many have stopped supporting and attending fashion week for that very reason. But the problem is this: If the few of us with limited access stop showing up, what representation will remain?

In 2018 Brianna McDonnell, founder of *The B Word* blog, was determined to find a way into the Christian Cowan runway show and, by manifesting that on her social media, was given a ticket at the last minute. With only a few hours till showtime, she opened her suitcase to find a sheer piece of white fabric that she'd thrown in there, unsure of how she'd incorporate it into a fashion-forward ensemble worthy of fashion week excellence. Before packing it, she'd spray-painted the word FAT across the garment several times. And then it hit her: this was her moment not only to embrace her fatness but also to wear it proudly on her chest in a room full of people who'd likely never been exposed to such exuberance and confidence before.

She cut a hole in the top of the fabric, draping it across her body, wearing a bikini top and fishnet shorts beneath. And then, glammed and prepared, made her way down to Spring Studios, resembling a gorgeously fat Norma Desmond come to life.

"I was nervous, but I wanted to do this," she says. "I want to be fat at fashion week, and this is the vibe."

As Brianna entered the room, her fatness quite literally on display for all to see, she immediately noticed only one other plus-size woman was in attendance: Lizzo. "I really wanted to go into a space that's very traditional in the language it uses, who's invited, who's seen, who's in the audience, and I wanted to say that I'm here and that other fat people should be here. We're taking that judgmental tone out of the word *fat*."

Reclaiming her power of the very word that was used to degrade and destroy her inner confidence since childhood was the reminder she needed that the work is always, despite trepidation, worth it. Because as segregating as fat or plus-size may seem, in moments like those, they remind you of the very community igniting your every step.

One thing's for certain: when we show up, we do so ready to embrace and tackle whatever stands before us. Gone are the days of hiding, of shrinking down to fit spaces that were never made to accommodate our bodies. Whether in attendance at fashion week, inside a designer's showroom, or simply posting on our social media platforms, we are rewriting the rules of this industry every step of the way.

7

REWRITING THE FANTASY

Had it not been for Victoria's Secret, I wouldn't have a fashion career.

In the fall of 2018 I was brought on as a freelance fashion news writer for *Teen Vogue*, eager to make my mark and work my way up from crafting shopping roundups to publishing forward-thinking exposés and op-eds. Fresh off a thrilling summer in New York City and the experience of my first fashion week, I returned to college that August with a new gig and a bright perspective. I then knew, without a doubt in my mind, that somewhere within this mess of an industry was a spot for me, for my voice. All I had to do was find it.

Between classes and study groups, I'd pull out my laptop and write daily stories for *Teen Vogue*'s website, everything from celebrity street style to brand collaborations. My studies quickly fell behind as I jumped on any opportunity to dive deeper into this oh-so-fascinating world of fashion and culture. And one day that November an opportunity came to combine my unique perspective with a major industry turning point: Victoria's Secret was burning.

In an interview with *Vogue*, the brand's then chief marketing officer Ed Razek made a series of comments disparaging and degrading marginalized communities, explaining why, from his perspective, they did not fit Victoria Secret's famed aesthetic. When asked about the lack of diversity seen during the brand's annual fashion show, his stance was made abundantly clear: "Shouldn't you have transsexuals in the show? No. No, I don't think we should. Well, why not? Because the show is a fantasy. It's a 42-minute entertainment special. That's what it is."

He continued by explaining that the brand sells to a specific customer, not the whole world, and that customer is one who checks few, if any, boxes on the list of possible identities. He ended his quote, "No one had any interest in it, still don't."

I'd beg to differ.

The backlash was immediate. Everyone from Gigi Gorgeous to Tess Holliday weighed in on the scandal. It's one thing to feel and know deep down that a brand doesn't believe you're worthy of being represented. It's another to be directly told so. Many wondered: If all that hatred could be spoken so confidently in public, imagine what's said in secret whispers.

"Victoria's Secret never cared about bodies like mine, so I'm not going to waste my energy trying to convince them that they should," wrote plus-size influencer Simone Mariposa. Phillip Picardi, the former head of both *Teen Vogue* and *Out* magazine, tweeted, "We, as an industry, must stop honoring this arcane pageantry and demand that they change. The fact that this show exists the way it does in 2018 is absurd."

That day felt like my moment to step in, to leverage my voice to its full advantage. I pitched my editor a feature speaking to six plus-size women about their triggering experiences with the brand. And when that piece went live, I received another email: the team at ThirdLove, a lingerie brand that had been specifically referenced in that *Vogue* interview, had decided to clap back, and they were giving me the exclusive.

Those two features solidified my role as a journalist and, even further, showed me the endless possibilities out there to expose this industry's hatred and turmoil of marginalized bodies.

In the days that followed, Fashion Twitter erupted in shared experiences of trauma at the hands of Victoria's Secret: From discriminatory shopping memories to the impact of the brand's infamous fashion show, it was all too clear: Victoria's Secret's reign had caused too much damage to go unnoticed. A new revolution had begun, and it was time to rewrite the fantasy.

For decades, the lingerie and intimates industries have promoted a dangerous, exclusionary fantasy, one that centers überthin, White women. Much of it has been built through the male gaze, creating imagery that fuels sexual fantasies at the expense of the very women it touts. Deemed unlikeable by men? Consider yourself irrelevant.

The shocking part is, however, that aside from a handful of dominating forces, many lingerie brands are in fact run by women who lean more conservative, as Cora Harrington, author of the book *In Intimate Detail: How to Choose, Wear, and Love Lingerie*, explains. "The industry itself is very conservative," she says. "Most lingerie brands are run and owned and designed by women. Even Victoria's Secret would have had women designers."

The exile of Victoria's Secret represented more than a singular brand's fall from grace. Rather, it ignited a much-needed conversation regarding the exclusionary model the lingerie world has operated upon for far too long. And for once, advocates across the industry could agree: this was an all-hands-on-deck battle.

Inclusive undergarments are crucial as they lay at the centerfold of everyday life for women and the folk who purchase them. An ill-fitting and even painful bra can make one's entire day feel like the tightest of hells. It doesn't matter whether your dress or jeans are made to flatter. Give a big girl a bra three sizes too small and nothing will feel right. It's a fact that everyone—across the spectrums of size, race, and background—can agree on, and is precisely why the conversation following that November's ruckus picked up steam so heavily.

The same is true for intimates. As Cora explains, lingerie has largely been painted as a heteronormative means to satisfy and pleasure one's partner. But the self-love movement has pushed to dismantle and rewrite that notion. Lingerie can, if one chooses, be a source of eye candy for another. But it should, regardless of that, make anyone feel confident and beautiful in their own skin. When done right, inclusive and masterful lingerie has the power to change how you view yourself.

That's especially true in the case of plus-size folk who have been told—by brands and designers and sexual partners—that they lack the capability to be "hot enough." First off, screw that. And second, that notion is the very thinking that kept brands like Victoria's Secret alive for decades. "If only I could look like *that*," women would wish, or "Maybe if I just lost enough weight to fit into *this*," they'd say, "maybe then men would love me and find me sexy."

Again, screw that, and if you'd been told that very message time and time again, you deserve *so* much better, and you already are so much better by simply acknowledging how archaic that mindset is. The false fantasy constructed by this industry serves a sole purpose: to alienate and ostracize anyone who deviates from what society deems beautiful.

"As a result of that lack of diversity, I think perhaps a lot of intimate apparel brands still think what's happening right now just isn't relevant to them," Cora says. "And you can see it in a lot of their websites, a lot of their copy, and in the models they choose. There's not really any innovation."

The technical side of bra design has its own set of challenges, as Cora explains. While many may feel that their desires are going unheard for years on end, the reality of the matter is designing a new bra—not solely in a different color, or by just adding a patch or an appliqué on an already-existing design—requires much more time than many understand. The lack of education on the customer side can often lead to anger and upset, understandably so as this woman has been denied well-fitting undergarments for decades.

"People don't know that a bra is supposed to make getting dressed easier," says Caralyn Mirand Koch, model and creator of the #ProperlyFittingBraClub. "Instead of standing up proud, your shoulders start to hunch and that affects your daily life, the way you carry yourself in conversations, your confidence."

Caralyn suggests getting fitted for bras at small business specialty shops, not major conglomerates. Chances are that local boutiques like those will be more inclined to take the time to understand your body and its needs, not simply pushing you to purchase their latest stylings. "No online quiz, no calculator, no virtual body scan will ever replicate in-person settings," she says. "There are so many incredible brands that are catering to women of all shapes and sizes. They may be a little bit harder to find, but they are out there, so don't lose hope."

Conversation is one of the best methods to find them. Ask those within your inner circle where they purchase bras and what their experiences have been. Direct-message influencers and advocates on Instagram, or read up on top industry blogs—like Cora's, for instance, which dives deep into both the customer and business perspective—to discover new launches that may cater to you. Half the battle is uncovering what's out there within reach.

Similarly, for the brands venturing into larger-size offerings, the process is multilayered. For starters, as Cora breaks down, a bra that is functional and not just for fashion purposes often takes much longer than six months to construct. It's not as simple as grading up sizes like in apparel design. With a bigger bust comes bigger support, wiring changes, and other subtle additional details. She's seen designers dedicate themselves to perfecting fit for new bra designs, only to scrap the project entirely when it didn't meet their hopes. "Because if you release the thing and it doesn't fit, that brings its own problems," she says. "And this is particularly heartbreaking for me. You have designers and brands create those new sizes, create those extended sizes, and then no store, no boutique, or department store picks it up, which is something I've seen happen a not-infrequent amount."

Then there's the issue of reach and exposure: A brand may extend its bra sizes, but without a massive website and following, getting the word out may be near impossible. The brand is left with no choice but to rely on the department stores that carry them, though customers may never come across those newly extended sizes.

Design is a process, after all, and expecting that a brand can flip from exclusionary to inclusive overnight is a bright-eyed fairytale. The logistics, however, are separate from the core values a company chooses to promote. Needing time to learn and expand is one thing; consciously choosing to promote only the most privileged and socially adored bodies is another.

"The whole concept of there being one ideal of sexy or that fantasy is not only wholly untrue, but it's so boring, so uninteresting," says model Michaela McGrady. "I love seeing people from all walks of life celebrated for their inherent sexiness and undeniable desirability."

In the hole created by Victoria's Secret's absence stepped forward a new generation of inclusive game changers ready to not solely elevate community but also prioritize them. Leading that revolution is none other than Rihanna and her Savage X Fenty line.

In its years since launch Savage X Fenty has pushed beyond the binary, celebrating Black beauty and true diversity in ways never before seen. You can always rely on Rihanna and her team to pull together the most beautiful spectrum of individuals, from those with disabilities to those of different heights, shapes, ages, and backgrounds. From e-commerce models to the brand's annual fashion spectacular, Savage X Fenty has shown that it's more than possible to be inclusive: it's profitable. Decentering the fantasy and filling it with authenticity is among the smartest moves a brand can make in the twenty-first century. And others have followed suit, from smaller brands like Curvy Couture to in-person experiences like the Real Catwalk, created by plus-size activist Khrystyana Kazakova.

In 2021, three years since its company-shattering moment, Victoria's Secret returned to the spotlight with a new initiative, one that eliminated the brand's famed angels and filled them with role models, including soccer star Megan Rapinoe, actress Priyanka Chopra, and model Paloma Elsesser, among others. Known as the VS Collective, this group of women are intended to serve as the brand's leaders and consultants as they push to a more all-encompassing future. And with new leaders hired internally— Razek resigned soon after those comments were published in 2018—the question remains: Can they recover? Can they regain the trust of the very women they rejected? Will they be celebrated for doing the exact thing women begged of them for decades? That answer depends on the consumer. But if anything, an intentional effort is finally being exerted, and it's certainly been noticed.

Meanwhile, however, I'll be watching the Savage X Fenty show on Amazon Prime, because that's the future I can see myself in.

"It is so empowering to walk around in a hot piece of lingerie and just feel like an absolute bad bitch," Michaela says.

Michaela came of age in the early 2000s when Paris Hilton and Nicole Richie ruled the universe—or at least, that's what reality television led one to believe. She recalls reading issues of *Cosmopolitan* that showed her—through the imagery on each page and the fatphobic words that followed—that thinness was the ultimate goal. It contrasted what she'd seen in her personal life, where the young men around her would appreciate and acknowledge women of diverse body types. "I was like, 'Wait, there's a disparity here. The media is trying to tell me that there's one ideal fantasy, one ideal of beautiful, one ideal of sexy, but the people I'm around are not reflecting that at all.'"

Suddenly, it all began to click. Her body wasn't the problem. Capitalism was. By using the media to make women like Michaela feel inferior, brands could sell them supposedly "surefire"—yet almost always useless—products to boost their attractiveness. Shapewear, body sculpting hacks, cosmetics—all of it was a ploy by diet culture to drain her confidence and bank account simultaneously.

For too long, fashion has operated on the same exclusionary model: Give customers not what they need, not even what they want, but what they can't have. Give them a holy grail to work toward, to aspire to. Something that will fuel their desire for "better," despite no true flaws in their current state of being. Make them feel unworthy under the guise of aspiration.

Aspiration versus inspiration: two words used interchangeably in the fashion world that should be differentiated:

In-spire (v): to fill an individual with the urge and passion
    to feel a certain way, sparking a desire for creativity.
A-spire (v): to center one's ambition on a certain goal or
    outcome.

Designers, for instance, feel moved to create unique collections season after season, drawing *inspiration* from various forms of life. Consumers, on the other hand, are pushed to *aspire* to become that fashionable, that stylish, that affluent, that thin. That is the very fundamental flaw that creaks within the foundation of the fashion industry. Clothing should, in my opinion, be used to inspire, as has been done often in the plus-size scene. It should fuel a person to want to reach their goals, to feel their best, to exert the most power on a day-to-day basis. Few believe that message will sell enough to keep the lights on.

Consumers are no longer passive shoppers. Rather, they crave feeling reflected and represented within the scope of a brand. This is particularly true for those of the plus-size community who have never felt that invitation before. Many designers refuse to give in to that desire, however, clenching firmly to the power dynamics at play that place them above the shopper as a stylish God prepared to dictate your every move. Widening the conversation to include the consumer brings that power balance to an end, and that is simply not how many wish to uphold their empires.

That's where the fantasy comes in: brands like the pretransformation Victoria's Secret decide to sell what the media, what society, what Hollywood has promoted as perfection, operating on the guarantee that body insecurities will last forever. What they never saw coming, however, was the day women would finally have enough.

These brands brainwashed us all. And they did an amazing job at it, until we fully understood our bodies have never been the problem. Their greed is.

Coming to that realization alone is difficult. It's why the online body positivity space is so electric, because people who have felt so alone, so lost, can connect with beautiful souls who will guide them through self-healing realizations. But having those bonds within the family is perhaps the strongest force of change one can experience.

Michaela—whose sister Hunter and mom Brynja both have had successful modeling careers—always felt that support growing up, and attributes it as the core of her confidence today.

"Our self-worth and a lot of our mental state starts at home, especially when it comes to empowerment and how we look at ourselves," she says. "My mom always said, 'Talking about weight is *so* boring.' That was so formative for me and my sister. . . . If more households operated that way, we would have a lot more healthy-minded people."

Dismantling the media's false fantasy on what equates beauty is often painted as a self-healing measure. But what's perhaps more important to recognize is that this work is not to make us feel better on an individual basis. Rather, it is so the next generation—our daughters, our nieces, our grandchildren—can feel that support, that love, and that acceptance as early as they can grasp it. Progress means nothing if the generation behind us doesn't feel its impact from birth.

For the girls who feel worthless, who believe their looks will never be good enough, for those who began to diet and starve themselves as early as elementary school, for the ones who wait outside the Victoria's Secret dressing rooms for their friends to finish trying pieces on, for the girls who feel like they could never be the next Heidi Klum or Naomi Campbell, for the ones who question whether life in this body is worth it . . .

You are the most beautiful, the most worthy, the most deserving. Because you can unlearn this fantasy. And you have the power to be your own supermodel.

"You are so beautiful, and you are so worthy, but you are also so much more than what you see in the mirror," Michaela says. "You are so much more than what the world wants to put value on. Your body is a piece of who you are, but it's not everything. You have so much more to offer this world. You are so beautiful, you are so sexy, you are so hot, you are all those things, but you are so much more than that." You are the fantasy, however you personally choose to define it. And that freedom to choose is the beauty that comes with true body positivity.

This concept of the perfect fantasy extends far beyond the world of lingerie. While varying among specific subsets of the industry, from beauty to bridal, its core remains unchanged: only thin, White, able-bodied, and affluent women are allowed.

Perhaps the most progress has been made in the beauty and cosmetics scene, with major brands and retailers prioritizing diversity in everything from their campaign imagery to shade ranges. And quite frankly, beauty should be the first to evolve. Makeup requires no specific size, no worry of fit. More issues lie in the shade ranges available, as until recently, the dominating makeup brands refused to cater to women of color, especially dark-skinned Black women, whose options dwindled for decades. Similar to fashion, however, the core essential remains: there is an ever-growing need to engage and satisfy this consumer in order to build a level of brand loyalty that many lack.

But as that obstacle has diminished, with more brands than ever expanding their shade ranges, *stigma* remains. If shade range is no longer an issue, and clothing sizes never played a role to begin with, why can't beauty be more inclusive?

There's no good reason, other than fatphobia and bigotry.

"They benefit from promoting ads that would make people feel inferior or insecure, to urge them to buy the product, instead of marketing it to enhance your beauty or get creative," says Hayley Herms, a model and popular beauty babe. Even when breaking the barrier and getting cast in various makeup and skincare campaigns, Hayley's found that sizeism lives on set as well. "They'll sometimes say tidbits like, 'Oh, are you the makeup artist?' And I'm like, 'No, I'm the model.' Or they'll say backhanded things like, 'So, is this your full-time job? Like you do this? This is what you do?'"

She adds, "Doesn't matter how famous you get, how established you are in your career. Whether it's the beauty or fashion industry, America is still very much pushing this agenda."

That limiting mindset has finally begun to expand as the data has become increasingly clear: Diversity sells. And the subsets of this industry that can cater to a wider spectrum of customers without having to rewire their entire frameworks have jumped on board sooner than most fashion brands ever will. Five years ago, the walls of a Sephora may have seemed like an insider's palace. Now, they're a come-as-you-are.

"Beauty is the first thing that fits," says makeup influencer Runa Azam.

Growing up, Runa found herself drawn to the makeup counter where, a majority of the time, products were one-size-fits-all. As the years went on and social media became increasingly popular, she felt inspired to join the online conversation, though "scared that no one would watch me because I was chubby," she recalls. Reigning the fear in, she took the plunge, and now more than seventy-five thousand followers later, one could say her courage has been well met.

Before social media stardom, however, Runa worked in management positions behind the counter at a handful of popular beauty destinations, including Sephora and Ulta. And when pushing back against corporate on why inclusivity was never made a priority, she was met with a simple response: those types of people don't buy. Runa reflects on what corporate would say: "'Black people, Indian people, Hispanic people, they don't buy.' They always made it seem like the highest purchaser was a White person. Everything was always so heavily marketed toward a White woman, that the rest of everyone was left out of the conversation."

She adds, "I would always be very shook and shocked that they would raise [such an issue] because here I am, a Bangladeshi girl, and half my paycheck goes into makeup. All my money would go to Mac because Mac was the only place that sold my shade. And I remember forcing myself to wear other brands at Sephora even though none of the shades matched me—there's so many pictures of me with a light face and my neck super dark—because I wanted to be in the beauty world so I could force the colors on myself."

If you don't invite *her* into the conversation, of course she won't shop. But even that disconnect can't deny the potential of buying power out there from marginalized communities. And the fight for inclusivity is far from over. The beauty world is capable of so much better. Bigger bodies, more ages, more shade ranges, better offerings—change is real, but change is not finished.

The same goes for the bridal industry, which—like lingerie and luxury and makeup—has promoted the same exclusionary model. Finding a plus-size wedding gown shouldn't be as difficult as it still is. Having to order custom, dealing with the widest range of fit issues, stuck with online-only offerings—I'll never envy the brides of today when it comes time for me to find my wedding day tux.

That issue is further rooted than simply believing fat folk can't be sexy and beautiful. Rather, it stems from the notion that plus-size women will never find love, never be desirable enough in the eyes of men. Why go through the trouble of creating luxurious gowns if the only role they'll ever play is that of a bridesmaid? Instead, even when approaching that special day, plus-size brides are encouraged to lose weight every step of the way. "Think about how you'll look in your wedding photos," they're told. "Don't you want to look your *best* that day?"

I'm not sure how many times I can say "screw that" this chapter, but allow me to scream it once more: *Screw. That.* We deserve to be the main character. We deserve to be the fantasy, or the antifantasy. We deserve to be as spectacular and incredible as our hearts desire, in whatever shape and form that takes. And we deserve to do so in an industry, society, and world that gives us the space to be free. Lingerie has never quite granted us that . . . until now. Finally, in our most intimate settings, we can let our curves breathe, giving them the sensitive touch of love they've desperately been craving.

The conversation around plus-size fashion often takes place on a grand scale, focusing itself on the top models or game changers in the industry. But at the end of the day, their work means nothing if everyday people aren't changed by it in the most normalized of ways. From putting on a bra every morning to playing around with the latest eyeshadow drop to looking dreamy at our weddings, true progress will be made when these simple, universally shared experiences are completely common and accessible for marginalized folk.

The day we'll celebrate is the day when all of this is normal.

8

LET US VOGUE

I F *THE DEVIL WEARS PRADA* TAUGHT US ANYTHING, it's that no one loves "skinny" quite as much as the Miranda Priestlys of the world. Thankfully, a decade and a half later, the Andy Sachses of tomorrow have taken charge.

As a college student during the peak of street style culture, Tyler McCall felt the only few who belonged in fashion media were the thin and wealthy—which, in many ways, still rings true today.

"When you don't see yourself reflected, it's hard to connect," she says.

She'd find her launching pad at Fashionista.com after cold-emailing upward of fifty editors at different major publications. And little did she know that just a few years later—with some jumping around in between—she'd rise the ranks to be the website's editor in chief. "I naturally started covering plus-size fashion because I was the only one who wasn't straight size that I worked with," she recalls, thinking back to those early intern days around 2012.

Tyler has had all the awkward experiences that come with being a bigger girl navigating the fashion industry's narrow lens, like uncomfortable press previews where she's been told, "Well, we go up to a size 10, but it's a *roomy* 10!"

"I swear to God, if I hear the phrase 'roomy 10' one more time in my life, I'm going to throw something out the window," Tyler says.

Then there's fashion week, when she'd show up super early to ensure there'd be enough room on the tightly packed benches for her. "I know my ass is wide, but we can do it, I believe in us," she jokes. Or simply—and perhaps worst of all—the feeling that being plus was detrimental to her career, constantly seeing only überthin women receiving promotions, mass attention, and top industry positions.

Don't be fooled. Conversations around body diversity in fashion *were* happening when Tyler started out. Madeline Jones, editor in chief of *Plus Model Magazine*, was a major proponent of that, opting to create her own opportunities for the community she loved so passionately. Her publication not only covered a wide spectrum of models and individuals from within the plus-size community but also gave exposure to those doing the hard work behind the scenes who had yet to be recognized on a grand scale. Once again, a catalyst would have to occur to push those important dialogues into the mainstream pages of *Vogue* and other famed fashion bibles. Much of that has only taken place in the past handful of years, right around the time I broke into the industry myself.

I often wonder how different my life would be if I had entered fashion just a few years earlier. I'd likely have no voice, no platform, no soul even. I'd likely be stuck working at a digital content mill, churning away articles about Amazon Prime Day and the latest lip gloss hacks, all while working for a salary below living wage. But as the print world began to suffocate and die in 2015 and the years that followed, the industry's battlefront attempt to keep itself alive included letting readers into the conversation, reflecting them on the page with the desperate hope they'd connect enough to hit subscribe. Would it be enough? For the most part, no. It would, however, give us some of the best representation we've yet to see.

Teen Vogue is living proof of that. The magazine, once a go-to destination for tween gossip, revolutionized its content, its leadership, its boardrooms, and its readers—my young and hungry self included—in a monumental way.

Upon graduating high school in 2015, I was left in a world of possibilities without a hand of direction. I'd spent the years prior deep in the world of musical theater, immersing myself in the dream of Broadway stardom. But without the support I needed to pursue such a challenging career from within my inner circle, I was left dumbstruck. Hopelessly lost, I'd given up on the idea of a life-changing college experience as I'd seen plastered in films, never even applying to my dream schools like Pace University and NYU. As I hung my cap and gown in the deepest depths of my closet that June, I was officially and utterly alone.

Few within my family understood the creative energy that'd been bubbling within me since birth. They relentlessly suggested I follow a career in the medical field, pushing two-year degrees in radiology or respiratory care. Others encouraged me to pursue computer sciences seeing as I was glued to my phone for most hours of the day. They failed to understand that my Internet obsession was rooted in the desire to escape and live a life far beyond the confines of their small-town mindsets.

With little time to decide and even less energy to care, I enrolled at a local community college to study as a paralegal. I thought, well, if Elle Woods could do it, then maybe so could I. Maybe I'd find my way, my "so much better" moment, within the complexity of legal jargon.

My first day of classes, I ate lunch alone in the bathroom Cady Heron–style. I cried in the parking lot later that afternoon.

I wallowed in self-hatred in my parents' basement that evening. As a creative outlet and a means to stay afloat, I launched a small theater blog in hopes of one day becoming a professional critic, a way to stay connected to the world of artistry I so passionately loved. I reached out to my town's top theater reviewer, Steve Barnes, who directed me on my way. Any former theater kid can tell you, there's not just a special place in your heart for theater. As you grow older and become more seasoned, you begin to realize the truth: theater is what keeps your heart beating.

My time blogging was the entertaining side hustle I needed to distract myself from financial accounting and business law courses. I quickly went from reviewing local productions to interviewing Broadway vets, and within the span of half a year, I was certain that this was my pathway: I was to become a theater journalist, even if only as a part-time job to supplement my paralegal work. It was enough to keep me content and keep me alive, and at the time, that's all that mattered.

Then, a few months later, I picked up an issue of *Teen Vogue*.

In spring 2016 the teen fashion and beauty publication brought in new leadership, naming magazine trailblazer Elaine Welteroth as its new editor. In the months preceding the 2016 presidential election, she and her adventurous digital team—led by Phillip Picardi—rewired *Teen Vogue* to be a magazine that reflected the desires, hopes, and conversations of teens today. Suddenly, articles on curling irons were swapped out for features on how to dismantle the patriarchy while wearing your favorite pair of jeans. And most intriguing to me was talk of a topic I'd never previously been exposed to: body positivity.

Any one of my friends during that time could tell you, I was *obsessed*. *Teen Vogue* became my big sister, guiding my every thought and action. She not only helped me form views on culture and society but also transformed the way in which I viewed myself on a personal level. I realized that there was far more to me than just a fat kid with a heart of song. There was a different person, a more realized person, waiting to break out on the inside. And *Teen Vogue* was there to guide me along the journey.

Teen Vogue's transformative revolution was met with widespread acclaim and appraisal from top journalism, Hollywood, and political names. At one point, the publication's website rose 200 percent in readership. Soon, another *Teen Vogue* gem caught my eye: a column titled Reclaiming My Size, all about plus-size fashion, written by Shammara Lawrence. I devoured it and was fascinated that a body like mine could matter within the larger fashion discourse. I had no idea that years later Shammara would go on to become not only my business partner but also my closest confidant. Though our *Teen Vogue* days are behind us, we'll never forget the fact that the magazine brought us together and shaped the people we grew to be.

Teen Vogue's revolution signaled much more than rising readership statistics; under its new direction, it showed the industry as a whole the possibilities that could be achieved by centering authentic, bold, and powerful voices. The publication's wellness and fashion editors—Vera Papisova and Jessica Andrews—lived by that, curating their teams and coverage carefully.

Anyone who knows me knows I can recite upward of one hundred Elaine Welteroth quotes off the top of my head. I credit her as my role model and her career as my roadmap, and my fascination with her excellence may sometimes teeter more on obsession than inspiration. One quote in particular stands out among the rest as the guidance I've operated according to: "You can't change the stories without changing the storytellers."

Nine simple words that ignited a revolution and changed a generation to come.

Inclusivity means nothing if not reflected behind the scenes. Welcoming in diverse hirings at the nation's top fashion magazines allowed the industry perspective to widen tremendously. And in the years that followed 2016, fashion media would catch on to inclusivity at a faster pace than ever before. Suddenly, diversity was not limited to the digital pages of *Teen Vogue*. It could be found everywhere. When Vogue.com began covering size-inclusive fashion launches, it was clear we'd broken the barrier. All of it was a major step forward, but there were miles to go.

"There are publications that are committed to it, and then there are publications that kind of do a precursory nod to inclusion but still elevate thinness and Whiteness as the physical ideal," says Samhita Mukhopadhyay, former executive editor of *Teen Vogue*. "To see how much things have changed in twenty years is really amazing. But whether we see that representation as much as we should? Not yet, no."

Samhita was brought into *Teen Vogue* in 2018 after Elaine's departure from the magazine. Her background as a renowned critic, author, and feminist force brought a deeper perspective to the publication, providing cultural and societal context to the important conversations the magazine continued to center. Watching from afar, I felt drawn and connected to Samhita, not solely because I was currently studying at her alma mater but also because she was one of the first plus-size folk to break the barrier. Samhita became someone I could both look up to and turn to when I needed it. Like one fashion week when, frustrated and helpless at how I'd been treated by PR folk, I approached her and asked for a title bump in hopes of being treated more seriously for the work I was trying to accomplish. I'd found that, despite my bylines and industry praise, none of it seemed to matter much without a fancy title to follow my name.

Representation does more than make one feel good. It allows you to step into your power, to take risks you'd otherwise never have the courage to take. If Samhita hadn't led by example at *Teen Vogue*, I perhaps would have never had the guts to request an in-person meeting at the Condé Nast offices that February—suited in white leather boots, a staple in Elaine's famed wardrobe—ready to walk away from the very career I'd been cultivating. But that day, Samhita guided me, reassured me, and handed me the support I needed to persevere through the cattiness that is fashion week hierarchy.

"Shallow representation does not actually lead to the types of deep cultural changes and cultural shifts that we really need," she says. Every editor, writer, designer, creator—we all have blind spots. That makes it all the more important for those depicting our society and documenting it in the media to be representative of the culture themselves.

Samhita adds, "To actually create equality in the workplace, you need to have editors that look like the changing face of America, and that's not just for bodies, it's for growing movements in this country around social justice and diversity."

The need for diverse storytellers extends beyond editors and writers. It means *all*, especially photographers whose imagery has the power to shape viewpoints in monumental ways.

Rochelle Brock, a size-inclusive photographer based in Brooklyn, NY, says:

Having people on set who understand what inclusivity looks like and how that manifests in different aspects of our life, how we are able to now showcase that, is really helpful to the cause. It allows for an environment that's more understanding, that's more aware.

When I'm working with models, seeing how they move their body, seeing how competent they are—that has helped me greatly with understanding my own body, helping even me be more comfortable in front of the camera. I kind of look outside of myself, and my work inspires me, too, and that's why I do it. Because I know how it makes me feel, and I know that when other people see it, they're going to feel the same way.

Some publications understand that better than others—like *InStyle*, for instance, which launched a plus-size-specific street style gallery during New York Fashion Week (shot by Lydia Hudgens) to increase visibility in a traditionally thin-only space. In my visits to various magazine offices over the past five years, from Hearst Tower to digital media startups, I've seen firsthand what the inner workings of these companies look like. And I could count on one hand how many prioritize diversity in the manner it should be treated.

"This is a top-down problem," says Gabrielle Korn, former editor in chief of *NYLON*. "This is a problem of a generation of people who don't understand that having runway models with body types that reflect 2 percent of the population is no longer what consumers want."

Gabrielle's time at *NYLON* was pivotal to the brand's resurrection. "I worked to make sure that size inclusivity was prioritized. And interestingly, we were up against more internal forces than external. People really wanted that content; the trolls paled in comparison to the people who always said, 'Thank you so much for representing me.'"

Fashion media is run by a toxic ecosystem dictated by advertiser dollars and clickbait velocity. It often matters less what you say or what stance you take and more how many readers care enough to click through. While editors may have jurisdiction on day-to-day matters, most major changes must be run through the gauntlet of old, White men who, without a second thought, will shoot down inclusivity initiatives as a matter of habit if they fail to guarantee a profitable return on investment. And that guarantee is nearly impossible to give unless a leap of faith is taken to establish a proven track record.

That's not to say editors don't have control. As made clear by Samhita, Gabrielle, Tyler, and women like them, change is completely possible when power is placed in the right hands. There's a ceiling, however, on how far they can go before advertisers and higher-ups get uncomfortable.

"There are not a lot of plus-size people in these rooms when decisions are being made," Tyler says. "I think there are people who don't realize that a plus-size person can't shop at Zara because they've never thought about it, because they've never *had* to think about it."

Samhita adds, "There's always an interest in putting the blame on one person or the onus on one person. Whereas really, it's a bigger ecosystem that has produced and perpetuated one type of beauty, and then that's reflected in history and culture and television and movies and magazines. And so it really is a bigger systemic thing."

Sometimes, however, taking the risk is worth the return.

I saw that firsthand in fall 2018 when, only a few weeks after the public crucifixion of Victoria's Secret, another high-profile brand was on display for all the wrong reasons: Dolce & Gabbana. The brand's founders, Domenico Dolce and Stefano Gabbana, received backlash for a campaign video that was deemed racist toward Asian women. The public discourse that erupted opened a can of worms on all the controversial and problematic statements they'd made in the past, from promoting the mindset that fat is deadly to stating that queer couples who adopt are building "synthetic" families.

I watched the dialogue around Dolce & Gabbana evolve quickly from my college in Upstate New York, refreshing my Twitter feed minute by minute to see whether I had something of value to contribute to the conversation. It was the day before Thanksgiving, and most editors at *Teen Vogue* had clocked out for the holiday. Feeling as though I had a scathing op-ed brewing within me, I emailed my editor with a pitch: "It's Time We Officially Cancel Dolce and Gabbana."

Within a minute, I received a reply: her out-of-office notice. I'd missed my chance. Or so I thought, until an hour later, when my email dinged: "Sure, I'd love to! Obsessed," she wrote.

With less than three hours to write, I crafted what remains one of my favorite pieces to this day. And under her guidance, I didn't hold back: this was my voice, my opinion, my perspective. It was a risk—I was a young writer, after all, going up against an industry leader, all under the protection of a media conglomerate that, until then, had supported the brand for decades.

Upon publication, the piece was met with online praise. But the best part came a year later, when over coffee, my editor told me something she'd forgotten to mention earlier: after returning to the office after Thanksgiving, Anna Wintour had offered her personal approval on the piece, in whichever Anna Wintour–way she operates.

We'd taken a risk. And it was approved by the queen of fashion herself.

Years later Dolce & Gabbana would reemerge in the fashion scene, dedicated to making things right for their past actions, even being one of the first luxury houses to expand their size ranges and support organizations like the Trevor Project. Whether they deserve support now is an individual choice consumers must weigh. But one thing's for certain: we spoke, we screamed, we stood up, and they listened. That's more than I can say for most brands.

Magazines no longer hold the same influence they once did. Rather than cultural indicators, they now serve more as inner-industry conversation starters. Readership is down across the general population, but designers and brands are still paying enough attention for these words to matter, or so one would hope. If anything, pushing to make the media more inclusive encourages designers to do similar, which in turn would have a direct influence on consumers. All of it is a cycle—a different cycle than the early 2000s when *The Devil Wears Prada* reigned supreme, but a cycle nonetheless.

"An investment in the plus-size community is not just making money off of them, it's putting money back into those groups by giving them jobs," Gabrielle says. "People want to see people who look like them. And we can say that until the cows come home. But until the executives making these decisions here listen, for me it's kind of like talking to a wall. It's obviously going to be about a new generation of people rising into power and making changes."

Amid the digital age, media has evolved to be less magazine-centric and more production based, with video, TV, and film taking centerfold as the cultural game changers. While a publication's reach may now be abysmal compared to twenty years ago, Hollywood's hand extends further than ever before. But just like in the print world, the same core values remain: storytellers have the opportunity—and responsibility, even—to change lives.

I've yet to feel fully represented and understood by a piece of television or film. Many can relate—Hollywood is making moves, but at a tediously slow pace. What's excited me most, however, is the evolution of a show that changed me and countless others: yes, *Project Runway*.

Like many reality shows, *Project Runway* has had its ups and downs, its groundbreaking seasons and its lackluster ones. But in 2015 the series celebrated an important first: a winning collection constructed entirely on plus-size bodies, made by plus-size designer Ashley Nell Tipton.

Ashley recalls her *Project Runway* audition coming at a crossroads moment in life, a time when she heavily questioned whether fighting the fashion industry's long-held beauty standards was worth the sweat. "I was up against so much at the moment," she recalls. Grieving the death of her beloved grandmother, Ashley decided to give the reality series her full shot, diving in with the hopes of reconnecting with that passion and spark she once felt toward designing. And she didn't hold back. In Ashley's audition tape she boldly categorized herself as being fun, funky, and fat, making it clear out of the gate that size was a point of conversation she brought to the table.

Throughout the competition, it was clear that Ashley was the "other" on set, often viewed at a lesser level for her commitment to size inclusivity, though it was that very dedication that landed her a spot on the show. "I automatically got the same feeling of being in high school and wanting to make people like me," she recalls. That became particularly clear one episode when the contestants were asked to explain who should be voted off, and all the other women chose her. It was a heartbreaking moment, and one of many emotional ones for Ashley during production. "I just remember [guest judge] Kelly Osborne looking at me and telling me, 'Don't worry.'" A few weeks later, Ashley would take home the win.

Her time on the show did more than expose size inclusivity to a new audience. It showed kids at home that regardless of their size, race, ethnicity, or background, they, too, could matter and reach the same levels of success as Ashley. Among industry kin, *Project Runway* may not hold the same prestige or level of influence it once did. However, for those located outside the fashion capitals of the country, it is often their first and only exposure to what our world looks like, even if bedazzled by reality TV magic.

While groundbreaking, Ashley's win wasn't enough to kickstart *Project Runway* into a public dedication of diversity. It would take a new class of creators to do so, and in 2019, when the show made the leap from Lifetime back to Bravo, the timing couldn't have been more perfect. New judges, new hosts, new mantras, the redone *Project Runway* is one that reflects what the fashion industry of tomorrow looks like, not the one of 2006.

"If you really want to be the future of fashion, you have to include everybody," says Nick Verreos, a former *Project Runway* contestant turned consulting producer who currently serves as the cochair of fashion design at the Fashion Institute of Design & Merchandising.

Bringing onboard Elaine Welteroth, Christian Siriano, and Brandon Maxwell, alongside previous judge Nina Garcia, the new *Project Runway* placed diversity at the forefront in a manner that should have been done years prior. Models of all races were selected, as were models existing beyond the gender binary. And plus sizes took a new position, too, with curvy models appearing every episode, rather than being reserved for those one-off "real woman" or "makeover" challenges. It was a huge commitment on the show's part, but one that Nick couldn't be prouder of. "There's no way back," he says. Throughout the casting process, he's seen firsthand that more designers than ever prioritize inclusivity in their brands. It's a refreshing take, he explains, especially for an LGBTQ+ man of color like himself who, when wanting to design growing up, felt a bit like a lost sheep.

That's not to say all contestants are fully onboard and prepared to design for curves. On the contrary, many struggle. Some scoff at the idea. The difference is that *Project Runway*'s new judges and hosts deny sympathy for those who refuse to do what we— our community—knows is the bare minimum. If designing for a size 14 gal is too hard to fathom, then perhaps designing for the future of fashion is not the career path one should pursue.

"They still struggle [with curves] and it's shocking because these gorgeous human beings will come in—the models—in these crop tops, sexy pencil skirts, high heels, showing their waist and their hips . . . and then designers want to just cover it all up," Nick explains.

It's moments like those that Elaine's words matter most: you can't change the stories without changing the storytellers. If *Project Runway*'s new creative team were to pass over those moments, to give grace to designers who feel like curves are just not a part of their aesthetic, they'd be doing disservice to the industry, to the next generation, and to the folks at home. "Of course, there are the fashionistas and the young fashion kids who want to watch it and dream to be on the show or be fashion designers. But for the most part, the audience is America, from the barista in Seattle to the brain surgeon in Detroit. That's the viewership."

And those are the folks who crave this message most.

Project Runway's evolution only scratches the surface on the new wave of authentic media representation changing the nation. Actors like Aidy Bryant and Danielle Brooks are breaking down Hollywood's beauty standards with every role and on-screen moment. Because they, like us, realize the power that comes with visibility.

As a society, we continue to underestimate the impact that imagery has on our minds. The filters, the photoshopping, the highlights—none of it is real. None of it is authentic. None of it is helpful. On the contrary, imagery and media that perpetuate false realities of what we should look like push us further and further away from the goal of self-love to embrace our bodies, our "flaws," our unique pieces of existence without the pressure to conform to what Instagram tells us is likable.

We each deserve so much better than what the media has fed us. We deserve *Vogue* editorials. We deserve red-carpet celebrations.

We deserve *inclusivity*. And step by step, we're getting there. It may take decades of dedication, infinite online screaming matches. But when the day comes that our televisions, our magazines, our Pinterest boards reflect us for who we truly are, that will be the day we breathe.

9

THE RACIAL DIVIDE

PLUS-SIZE FASHION OFTEN operates under the false guise of exemplary inclusivity. From the outside looking in, all is puppy dogs, rainbows, and cold shoulder blouses. We're labeled as fashion's safe haven, a subset of the industry that has escaped this world's hatred, elitism, and various forms of segregation.

Ask any Black woman and she'll tell you how grossly incorrect that assumption is.

Like the fashion industry at large, the plus-size world is rife with racism, colorism, and anti-Blackness. It's harrowing given how essential Black women have been to the creation of this very movement. Yet as size inclusivity has moved mainstream, the folk who originally fought to dismantle these antiquated beauty ideals are too often erased from the conversation.

"Body positivity has become a mainstream idea, and with that, a lot of thinner, lighter-skinned bodies have become the face of the movement," says influencer Simone Mariposa. "We have a lot of smaller women hunching over or twisting their bodies to create rolls, and in that, we forget about the women, especially the Black women, who have rolls 24/7."

Progress over the past decade has given us much to celebrate. Gone are the times when body positivity solely existed in secluded corners of the Internet. Now, plus-size models grace the covers of *Vogue,* and designers like Versace have pushed to reevaluate who is "deserving" of their designs. As the momentum has intensified, however, certain voices and stories have been left behind, lost within the shadows of those rising the ranks to stardom. More often than not, those excluded and exiled are the very women of color who laid the foundation for this work to even occur.

"I believe in being inclusive, but I also believe in understanding our differences and that we're all coming from different places of oppression and different levels of marginalization," Simone says. "[Black women] are already coming from below. We're just trying to get to sea level, at that. And instead of it being let's uplift Black women and [fat Black femmes], it becomes, 'Well, why don't you want to uplift us *all?*'"

As the conversation around racism in the industry has intensified, many White folk and non-Black POC have reflexively questioned why centering Black women is so vital in a movement that is now for *all.* They acknowledge that while Black women may be at the core of body positivity and fat acceptance, the message has now expanded to encompass all bodies, all backgrounds, all people. That thought might hold more significance if at any point in history Black women were paid their dues for the backbreaking work they've accomplished. But the fact of the matter is, the moment that body positivity went mainstream, rather than elevate the women of color holding up its pillars, capitalism kicked in and instantly gave credit and checks to popular White folk preaching self-love. "Whenever there is money to be made, there are White people around," says writer Jess Sims. "That is a fact of life."

According to activists, what needs to be done is far more than a simple acknowledgment of who precisely created the groundwork for what we have today. What is *deserved* is more than that. It's reparations, equity, and equality, Jess says. To argue otherwise is to ignorantly silence the very women whose labor you're profiting from.

In her personal experience, Jess has found that fatphobia operates uniquely within Black communities. In Black spaces fatness may be a source humor. She recalls classic bullying around her size growing up, being made fun of and poked at for her weight. In White communities, however, she notes that until recently—and perhaps even today in certain circles—fatness is ostracized. White folk are terrified of being fat and the implications that come with living in a larger body. "White people treat fatness like a moral failure. We [in the Black community] treat it just as a by-product of life."

The root of that disparity can be traced back all the way to the days of slavery when antifatness and anti-Blackness sprang up from a single nexus of hatred. What we deem to be fatphobia or antifat bias today stems from the ways in which Black women were both treated and viewed centuries ago, their bodies categorized as failed attempts at controlling animalistic appetites. As explained in depth by Sabrina Strings in her groundbreaking book *Fearing the Black Body: The Racial Origins of Fat Phobia*, everything from broad societal views to medicine has been influenced by the dehumanization of Black folk.

For centuries, White people have tortured the Black community for their physical features. It is why White folk fear fatness extraordinarily more, because their disgust behind bigger bodies is directly tied to the disgust around Blackness which, in our racist society, equates to the state of being worth less. "In mainstream white society, being fat is akin to being evil," Jess says. "A white girl told me once when I was seventeen years old: The worst thing a man could be is short. The worst thing a woman can be is fat."

This twisted truth is beyond evident as we've seen beauty ideals evolve through the Kardashian era. Whereas once Black women were brutalized for their curvaceous shapes, now those very bodies are sought after through surgical measures. In mainstream culture, hips were horrendous until Kim Kardashian got herself a pair, and like in most aspects of life and fashion, it took influencers like Kim to make Blackness White enough for it to be deemed desirable.

As many fat activists, like Jess and Simone, have noted, Black women, fat femmes, and queer folk of color are the blueprint for plus-size fashion. They inspire the trends, the conversations, the momentum. They put their careers and lives on the line for change—like those in the 1960s who launched the fat acceptance movement. And still, to this day, they're rewarded with scraps.

The racial divide from within the plus-size space has become abundantly clear. Brands have failed this community as much as this community has failed itself. Many were quick to post black squares to their Instagram in solidarity during the height of the Black Lives Matter movement in 2020, though their posts were often deemed not enough to look beyond past actions. If it took a nationwide uprising for brands, influencers, and self-proclaimed "advocates" to finally pay attention, then clearly a listening ear has never been of importance.

Acknowledging one's privilege only goes so far. Recognizing personal advantages in this industry and society as a whole is a baby step to working toward being a true ally. It's about so much more than hearing Black and marginalized voices. To do better, they must be elevated and prioritized in spaces that have remained White-only for decades. For designers, that means expanding the spectrum of Blackness and models of color showcased in your collections. For influencers, it means forgoing opportunities to those who are most deserving, or who, despite having accomplished the same amount of work, have never been awarded the chance. Equality can never be achieved through word of mouth. To get there, we must open our minds, our souls, and our checkbooks to the very women and folk we've allowed this industry to displace and abandon since its origin.

Many, however, would rather continue to center themselves while doing just enough social media activism to satisfy their online followings.

Brooklyn-based model and writer Kendra Austin observes:

> [These people] don't perpetuate an image or language that threatens White supremacy, they are never saying, "White women, this is not for you." They are never saying, "The work doesn't just stop at loving yourself; we are dismantling fatphobia, which is connected to classism and White supremacy." They are never saying, "You need to be reading *Fearing the Black Body* by Sabrina Strings." They are never offering actual information, because once we dig into the history, they will have to give up their space on the platform. And ultimately, this is White supremacy, and White supremacy operating as narcissism within one individual human being on a grand and very personal scale on social media.

Some performativity and missteps as brands and influencers catch up is understandable, if not inevitable. There's no singular right way to be an activist or ally. And even then, to do so requires a deep education. No one should be forced to speak on topics they've not had the chance to see through their own eyes to form a fully informed perspective. The issue comes, however, when popular influencers build their platforms entirely off oppression and societal hatred toward plus-size bodies, only to then not acknowledge the political aspects that come with it once they've reached financial comfort.

Perhaps the first step we can all take to bridging this racial divide is elevating the trailblazing women of color who have never properly been given the time of day. Among them is Liris Crosse, the *Daily Mail*'s crowned "Naomi Campbell of Plus."

Growing up, Liris always loved having her picture taken. She recalls one moment when, during her father's campaign election for Congress, a photographer asked to capture her specifically. Returning two weeks later with her print in hand, he told Liris's parents that her photogenic nature would make her the right fit for modeling. That day wasn't enough to launch Liris's star quite yet, though it did plant the seed for her extraordinary career to come.

Venturing into middle and high school, fashion continued to weave its way into young Liris's life, whether through literature, reality television, or the occasional for-fun runway show. With that photographer's word cemented in mind, she decided to take a chance and attend a local modeling convention, participating in her first casting call.

The result: callbacks from four major agencies.

The issue: they all wanted her to lose weight.

"This was me now being in high school, a full-time year-round athlete. So it was like, lose weight? Where?" Liris recalls. She obliged, however, and shed a few pounds before the next casting call came around. Imagine her shock when, despite following orders, she received even fewer callbacks. With modeling then on the back burner, she applied and registered for college. But just a short time before the start of the session, she felt a call to action from within. She owed it to herself to give her dream a shot, to move to New York City and show the modeling industry that they were wrong about her, that her voice and body mattered. With the support of her parents, she pulled out of college and headed to the Big Apple.

After being told to lose weight by agents countless times, Liris was finally connected with an agent specializing in curve modeling. Seeing this as her way into the industry, she signed on the dotted line. And in just a few years' time, her star began to rise to heights few fully realize.

Liris's career has been filled with top-tier moments: walking in Lane Bryant's first lingerie show; shooting fashion campaigns with Queen Latifah; appearing in *MODE* magazine; shining bright in films like *The Best Man*; working in the video game industry; writing her own book titled *Make the World Your Runway: Top Model Secrets for Everyday Confidence and Success*; and perhaps her most well-known accomplishment, being the first plus-size woman to win the model portion of *Project Runway*.

Despite an extraordinary career, many argue that Liris—like other Black women—has not been paid her rightful dues. I whole-heartedly agree. Liris says:

> When there's only one spot [for a job], that means there's also this level of elitism within our industry. You might have all the goods: You might have the skin, the body, the charisma—all of that stuff. But if you're not signed [to one of these major agencies], you're not even being called for that job. If most of the Black girls are not able to get on the board of some of these big agencies that are able to get the high caliber job that we need, how are you going to see that Black girl? Being a model is hard, then being a Black model is hard. And when you want to add plus on it?

Liris recalls one experience when, after shutting down the show at Full Figured Fashion Week, she approached the head of marketing at a well-known plus-size brand that she'd worked with extensively years prior. In response, she asked Liris which agency she was now signed to, having left her previous group. And upon Liris's response, this well-known executive asked if there was any way she could head off and get signed to the industry's top agency instead. "Why do I have to get with [that specific agency] for you to book me? If I have the look and the ability to do it, you should just book me. I've proven myself, and I've worked with your company before."

She adds, "It makes it hard because sometimes these agencies have a monopoly. Now they're getting more diverse, but a few years ago, you could look at some of these modeling boards and they would only have one or two Black girls, and the rest would be White."

Despite these obstacles, Liris remains a force within the industry. Her mantra to "stand in your power" is evident in every move she makes, from the jobs she books to the manner in which she passionately speaks. For me and countless others, Liris is our supermodel, and even further, our superwoman.

She reflects:

> When I step in the room, I'm standing in my power; I'm standing in full confidence of who I am, what I bring to the table. When you respect yourself, when you honor yourself, people feel it, people sense it, people gravitate towards it. People have to let their light shine in the full awesomeness of who God made them to be. And all the capabilities and all the things that make them unique, from the freckles on their face to their beautiful nappy curls. Stand in that power. Stand in that awesomeness.

Modeling agencies often dominate the representation conversation. While newer agencies have been regularly booking diverse models for retail jobs, the biggest of gigs—the fashion weeks and luxury campaigns—are almost always granted to the industry's top model leaders. It's not always a matter of talent, and more often an issue of access. A few years back, a quick glance through the boards of these top agencies would reveal a huge failing on their part: of the few—*very* few—curvy Black models represented, almost all were biracial or racially ambiguous. An important identity to spotlight but not the only Black woman needing representation.

As a society we make little room for the conversation around biraciality, especially within the plus-size fashion space. In the loud social media sphere, mixed-race models are often told they're not Black enough to represent the community at large, while the industry still categorizes them as "too Black" to book certain high-level gigs. It's a tricky position to navigate: many of the firsts in Black history have come from biracial people, like President Barack Obama, Tracee Ellis Ross, and Zendaya. Their success is often linked to their proximity to Whiteness. They push racial boundaries—enough to make history, but not enough to make White folk uncomfortable. Acknowledging how the world and fashion industry upholds colorism in this regard is crucial to dismantling toxic mindsets. The flip side is, however, that this often leaves biracial folk at a challenging crossroads that feels minimizing to their unique identities.

Kendra notes how her biraciality makes her an "inherited benefactor of colorism":

> Generally in high fashion, there are rarely actually any women that look like me. I'm talking about hair; I'm talking about texturism; I'm talking about skin tone—because I look like a Black American woman. And when we're selling art, nobody wants Black American women, because that's seen as low class, this is seen as attainable, that is seen as nonaspirational, which is what high fashion is.

The opportunity to tell my truth as a human being is taken away because I can't tell the Black story, but I can't tell the White story either. . . . Rather than just making the critique of, "Let's notice the patterns of how a lot of these people that are granted first or getting proximity are biracial, and let's now grant space to more," versus "Let's take this opportunity from these people." . . . We should just create more room. But instead, we're kind of still operating in that scarcity, that Whiteness and capitalism tells us that only a few can have it.

As you begin to dive further into these various intersections, it becomes abundantly clear how multilayered the conversation is. It's one that cannot be solved through Twitter battles or the occasional Instagram Live session. Together, we must find a way to acknowledge one Black experience while making substantial room for others. Dark-skinned Black women—particularly those on the higher end of the size spectrum—are often the least represented within fashion owing to their multiple intersectionalities. The industry itself seems only capable of handling one identity at a time, which lends itself to terrible tokenization. Having one-of-a-kind is progress, but how far can it really move us?

"Just this year, thankfully, we've been seeing brands put on people like Precious Lee, which has been amazing to see a woman with darker skin tone being involved in high fashion," says Jazzmyne Jay, an influencer and diversity consultant. "But there are plenty more where that came from, and also women that are bigger than her that also deserve these opportunities."

Just as there is a whole range of plus-size experiences to pull from, there is a whole spectrum of Blackness that deserves to be represented within fashion. It should never be one or the other as this industry has sadly made it out to be. That is where conversation, critique, and allyship come into play. Those with the privilege and platforms to do so should encourage brands and designers to look past their limited views and embrace the spectrum of bodies and lived experiences just waiting to finally feel seen. Tag them, message them, email them. Whatever it takes, remember that the fight cannot be won alone.

"There is a time where as an ally you need to use your voice and think about what you're saying and how you can help other people," Jazzmyne says. "But also, there's a time where you need to be self-aware to let other people talk . . . because the main thing about being an ally is literally decentering yourself."

For those like community organizer Danni "AmaPoundcake" Adams, activism and allyship mean little when reserved for online-only spaces. "What our community has to do is believe and understand that we cannot get to liberation with only online activism," Danni says. "We have to do the real community work."

And according to her, that goes beyond simply advocating for change in the fashion space. It means attending city council meetings, speaking out for fair housing and shelter, exposing wage discrimination, dismantling medical fatphobia, and pushing back against fatphobic practitioners. Fashion is fun, but there's a whole world out there that still makes life as hard as can be for fat Black folk, and doing the tangible, hands-on work to change that is what constitutes allyship for Danni.

"We deserve a quality life beyond clothing. I want to look good, I like to dress nice, but I also want to be able to go into a hotel in a bed that accommodates my body. I want to be able to fly with an airline and not have to pay for two seats. That's the area where we're missing what it takes beyond social media to enact change for our community."

Some—like Jess—have a difficult time with the concept of allyship, having been let down time and time again by folk who claim to support the causes at hand but who never follow through in meaningful ways. If there's anyone who's been abandoned innumerable times by this industry, it's Black women. "The cognitive allyship by and large to me is not real. Because really, what you want to do is put a black square up on your Instagram and put BLM in your bio [and call it a day]," she says.

Similar is true for popular plus-size fashion brands that, until recently, have failed the very women feeding their bottom lines. Jazzmyne adds, "Usually [when you ask about diversity], you get that runaround of, 'We know, we're working on it.' How many times have we heard 'we're working on it'? Respectively, I have seen how long things do have to take to [come to fruition]. But at the same time, if people want it to be done urgently, they get it done urgently."

While racism remains rampant throughout fashion today, more work is being accomplished behind the scenes. Makeup artists, photographers, and stylists of color have begun to break through the door at a faster rate, largely thanks to the many models who have spoken out about how alienating it is to be the only Black person on set. "They make us feel like our Blackness is terrible for their brands," says influencer Sabrina Servance, star of Lifetime's *Big Women: Big Love.* "There's nothing more awful than trying to work in a space where people are complaining about your hair as if you're not there, and speaking about your hair in a way as if it's a detriment to what they're trying to produce."

Black women bear the brunt of this industry's most hateful moves. They are rejected and ignored, only until they are needed to step in and educate. While social media has helped to reveal the disgusting ways in which they are often treated, it's also placed pressure on the Black community to constantly speak out, speak loud, and solve the deepest world issues. "Black women are expected to do the work, and White women are expected to be beneficiaries of the work," Kendra says. In an effort to understand the Black experience, White folk often demand emotional labor from people of color, begging them to explain, to educate, to introduce them to the most emotional of topics. And for some, particularly fat activists, they take those opportunities to make real change on a direct level. Others, however, feel that burden is too difficult to hold. Why should they, the very people subjected to this industry's systemic racism, have to put in extra (note: often unpaid) work to educate folk who, until recently, showed no interest in learning more?

"I think that Black women continue to be the Mammy figure online, and continue to uphold this standard of being all-knowing, omniscient, omnipresent, omnipotent," Kendra says. "Someone who tells them what is right and what is wrong. It reminds me of that very 2014-like printed T-shirt that said, I've MET GOD, SHE'S A BLACK WOMAN.'"

Existing in a fat, Black body is inherently political given society's continuous maltreatment of these communities. The issue arises, however, when folk feel forced to speak out and constantly be teachers on these issues. Whether certain Black women in fashion choose to use their platforms for educational activism is an individual decision, and not something that should be demanded from White folk who most likely have not taken the time to research these topics themselves.

The unfortunate truth is that a clear racial divide remains within the plus-size community today. It's disheartening to experience this from a brand and designer perspective. It's worse to live it from within one's own community.

If the past three decades have taught us anything, it's that change is best accomplished together. Because together, we are a force. It was many women of the 1960s who screamed fat liberation in the most difficult of spaces. It was many women of the early 2000s who brought *MODE* magazine to life. It was many women who broke down the barriers to the top modeling agencies, demanding they represent curvy bodies. And it will be many women, men, and trailblazing folk who do the same to pay Black women their dues. Not on an industry level, not on a high-fashion level, but on a personal one.

"I actually don't hope to impact fashion, I don't think that fashion is something that can be penetrated," Kendra says. "I hope to impact the hearts of the people who consume fashion. Because those people are worth saving, and they can be saved."

ROUNDTABLE

MASCULINITY AND TRIUMPH

A NEW FRONTIER LIES AHEAD: The battle for size-inclusive mens-wear. It's a slow fight, one that's lacked the momentum needed to push it into the mainstream. But for men like me, it's what consumes our every waking thought: When will *we* have part in the celebration?

Two folk who inspire me deeply are Mina Gerges and Marquis Neal, models and content creators who are some of the only fighting to widen the inclusive conversation to include *us*. They've taken matters into their own hands, and with that, they have created some of the most beautiful and safe communities to be a part of.

Here are their stories.

This interview has been edited for clarity and length.

Why do you believe we've seen a lack of progress and momentum when it comes to size-inclusive menswear?

Mina Gerges: Fatphobia is something that's taught to men at a very young age. It is something that even to this day we're so conditioned to believe that way that no one is challenging it. When you think about men who work in the fashion industry, they see this huge lack of clothing and visibility for bigger guys, but they don't want to do anything about it because they don't find it attractive or don't think men should be like this. So it's people's personal beliefs that are really preventing our visibility from becoming a norm in fashion.

Marquis Neal: Yes, we are normal people, and we see people of our size all the time who work in the fashion industry, they still are ingrained to think that we are supposed to perpetuate that toxic narrative. They believe that plus-size men especially should not particularly be stylish and that they should desire to be, for lack of a better term, more "masculine," whether that means working out more, being more "healthy." And I don't think many have challenged them until now.

MG: I think it's also easier to look at the thin male silhouette and think that is the only fashionable type of silhouette out there. So no one is actively trying to create clothes that cater to our shapes and our curves and anything like that, and they don't want to because if they don't think that fat guys are a standard of beauty in the first place, then why would they create products that cater to something that they don't think is attractive?

On a personal level, what has helped you both to dismantle these toxic stigmas for yourselves, and to create space to blaze your own trails?

MG: Seeing other people, like Marquis, reject those notions creates confidence in me to keep doing these things. Growing up and being taught to feel ashamed of my body my whole life, I really am sick and tired of being made to feel like my body is a problem. Going to the mall, for example, it's kind of really fucked up that I can't even shop at a Zara or H&M like most people do. It's so dehumanizing to think that there's an entire industry that doesn't believe that you should get dressed up or that you should be stylish, so that fuels me to create my own content and representation.

MN: For me, it's about creating things and scenes and visions and moments of opportunity and inspiration for people to identify with until it reaches those industry higher ups. There is so much more that should and needs to be represented, whether it's just through fashion or other marketing, so we have to create it.

As models, are you beginning to feel more accepted within fashion spaces, or do you still feel very othered?

MG: There's a lot of me having to give myself a pep talk, not just to remind myself that I deserve to be there, but to also mentally and emotionally prepare myself to hear certain things that are said on set that are really not that okay. Usually something is going to happen that's going to hit your confidence or make you realize that you are different, and you have to prepare for that. At fashion events, I feel pressure to step up my style game because not only do they not expect you to be there, but they also don't expect that you would dress really well or look incredible. You feel like you have to prove that not only do you deserve to be there, but that you are on par with all of the other skinnier models.

MN: The pep talk is key. I always have to remind myself that *I* got the job. It's hard on set when people are conditioned to make jokes about their weight without also reading the room of other people there. I'm the only fat model here, and you're berating your body. So it is a constant game of reminding yourself that you belong in that room.

What is your vision for the future of fashion?

MG: I think the common theme with all three of us, and even just the direction that fashion is going into, is really about creating the representation you always wanted to see. We're putting matters into our own hands, and that shows the resilience of this community.

MN: It's beautiful that we are in an age now where if someone doesn't want to cast me in their campaign and I want to put that energy into something, I can create content to quite literally show the brand what they're missing out on. It's the most amazing thing to be able to know that I am the one that has the agency; I'm the one who's creating the marketing; I'm the one who casts myself as the role. I'm not tokenizing myself. I'm not placing myself in clothes that are smaller than what I actually wear. It is incredible to know that we as a community are able to write our own narrative.

MG: It's safe to say that every man has grown up with body issues, and if you're gay, that is definitely something you've experienced. So what we're talking about and what we're pushing for is not something that is this novel concept that they don't know about. I think it's common knowledge, but there's still the disconnect. And that's what I hope the next step is: it's not just about representation, but there's this system that excludes certain people from being able to find clothes that fit them, and that core needs to be dismantled.

MN: The future for me looks like there being no limitations in the fashion industry in terms of sizing. I just hope that the industry realizes beyond clients, beyond market, beyond consumer, that we're just people that want to get dressed. There's nothing more empowering than just being able to get dressed and feel good about yourself.

MG: I hope the future of men's fashion is more brands recognizing the need to create extended sizing, and understanding that it's not just about consumers. It's about really creating options for all men, as opposed to some men. I hope that the fashion industry overall just wakes up to the fact that there's real harm that's done in creating clothes that are so small and that don't fit certain sizes. Part of what makes fashion so beautiful is allowing people to express who they are, and by limiting the amount of sizes you sell, you are saying that you don't believe that this entire group of people is worthy of feeling good and being who they are.

10

THE BRAWN BOYS

ADY DEL VALLE'S FASHION ORIGIN STORY is made for the movies. As a young Puerto Rican growing up in Boston, he remembers blasting music through the halls of his childhood home, strutting those makeshift catwalks in his mother's garments. In high school, he'd stock up on issues of *Vogue* and *Elle*, tucking them beneath his bed at night as if they were guilty pleasures. Little did Ady know that years later, his face would grace the same editorials that once fueled his passionate soul.

"I've always loved fashion," Ady says. "But it never crossed my mind to become a model because I thought that didn't exist for me or for people like us."

That *us* is plus-size men, the big boys who, until now, have never felt like body positivity pertained to our distinct struggles. The size-inclusive menswear market of today stands years behind in progress compared to the women's sector. And understandably so; it's a newer arena, after all. Women have been fighting this fight tirelessly for over three decades while men have only recently come on board. Yet upon analysis, while many of our hurdles are similar beyond gender lines, a handful of unique challenges lay in the details as to why plus-size menswear has felt frozen in time.

Through the media and Hollywood, bigger men have been painted with a broad, inaccurate stroke. Popular sitcoms depict them as slobs, lazy individuals, and unsuccessful, unmotivated beings. They are either comedians or the brunt of comedy. And while plus-size men have been showcased in the mainstream vastly more than women over the decades, it's not particularly positive or encouraging representation.

Thankfully, a new wave of warriors is assembling to change that. They are what the modeling industry has deemed as *brawn*—another word for plus size, big and tall, husky, and the like—and leading them is Zach Miko.

Zach's introduction to the world of modeling happened by accident. Pursuing film and television in New York City, he was a bit perplexed when his commercial agent sent him a casting call for Target. He'd done some print work before, mostly for brands like Geico and ESPN. But a fashion gig? That was new territory. Skeptical, Zach didn't think too much of it, heading to the casting soon after with an open mind. And when the clothes just didn't fit—"None of them fit. None of them came even close to fitting," he recalls—he walked away certain that that was the end of the road.

Two hours later, he received a call from his agent: he'd booked it.

The day of the shoot, Zach ran into the same troubles: "They did not have samples to come even close to fitting me. The stylist that day had to literally cut and sew and kind of Frankenstein it onto my body to take the shots."

Despite that, however, the Target team was quickly drawn to Zach, hiring him multiple times over the next few months. And one day, while scrolling through his Facebook feed, he'd come across an article written by Bruce Sturgell of Chubstr.com: "Did Target Sneak in a Plus Size Male Model?"

Shocked to see his body plastered across the piece, Zach reached out directly to Bruce, connecting and conducting an interview between the two that would go viral. Soon Zach's work would be featured everywhere from *Good Morning America* to the *New York Post*. It was only a matter of time until Ivan Bart, president at IMG Models & Fashion, slid into Zach's DMs. Having led the charge for curve modeling in the industry, Ivan believed IMG's next natural step was to reflect that level of diversity in their men's division as well. And while Zach originally thought his Instagram message may be a scam, he agreed to a meeting, and all of it felt quite serendipitous.

"It was the next step for us, recognizing all beauty and all walks of life, and including that in the talent that we represent," says Josh Stephens, senior manager at IMG. With the launch of the agency's brawn division in March of 2016, the start of a new market and movement was well underway. But progress would be much slower than one would hope.

"It was still one of those things where there wasn't an industry yet," Zach explains. "There wasn't a market. There was nowhere for me to model. The clients who even did have big and tall didn't even have samples for actual big and tall guys. So it was a very weird situation of trying to make it all work."

Much of that initial work involved deep behind-the-scenes conversations, attempting to show brands the potential out there to represent a whole spectrum of men who had never been welcomed into fashion. Slowly but surely, they'd come on board one by one. Still, no designer was quite ready to make capital *F* fashion in a size fat for bigger men. We'd be given scraps first, just as our female cohorts had endured years earlier. Flannels, chinos, polos, button ups—none of it was quite revolutionary, but it was progress, and that was enough to keep the conversation moving.

The deeper issue was—and still is—that not just designers needed to be convinced that plus-size men matter. Those very men needed to believe it.

"Guys were raised with this 'Boys don't cry, boys don't show emotion, boys can't let other people know their feelings' mentality," Zach explains. "Because of that, guys who did have insecurities about themselves or their bodies or wanted more out of the fashion industry stayed silent, they didn't complain, whereas the women's industry over the last thirty years has been pushing and growing and supporting one another and demanding more."

Before we can change the industry, we must change ourselves.

Toxic masculinity runs rampant through society today. Young boys are taught that the only way to be "man enough" is to exert optimum strength, confidence, and power. Any deviation from that is a sign of weakness or failure. Step out of line and suddenly, your masculinity card is revoked. This is especially true for bigger boys who struggle with twenty-first century body ideals. From Zac Efron to Hugh Jackman and every Hollywood heartthrob in between, being "man enough" requires a body so ripped, chiseled, and flawless in the eyes of society that it warrants a centerspread in *Men's Health* magazine.

Big boys may never achieve that. Studies show that as more weight is added to the body, traditionally masculine features— such as a sharp jaw, chiseled facial features, and pecs—fade away, feminizing certain parts of the body. It pushes the notion that masculinity is solely a reflection of one's outward appearance, rather than an internal spectrum and equation.

"For me growing up, my options were to get a six-pack or to be the fat funny guy," Zach says. "Those were the two roles you were allowed to have. And I tried doing both: I never got a six-pack, never came close to getting a six-pack. And I tried to be funnier. I think I have a decent sense of humor, but I'm no comedian or anything like that, so I struggled with finding who I was."

This, however, is different when race is involved. A 2013 study titled "Masculinity, Competence, and Health: The Influence of

Weight and Race on Social Perceptions of Men"—conducted by three researchers from SUNY Buffalo, the University of Houston, and the University of California, Riverside—found that while thin White men are perceived to be smarter and more competent than thin Black men, the opposite is true when it comes to men of a larger size.

Beyond the physical is the battle to conceal one's true emotions. Men are statistically less likely to open up about issues like body image, eating disorders, and body dysmorphia out of fear of being deemed fragile. And while it may be trendy for TikTok teens to state how attractive a man that is in touch with his emotions is, pay close attention to the very guys they point to. Tears may now be acceptable in certain circles if outwardly you present as the pinnacle of manhood: Timothée Chalamet's tears are golden drops of purity; Kevin James's are humorous.

And then there is society's demeaning view of fashion as a female-only conversation. Body positivity is "girly" enough. Imagining a group of men sitting around the kitchen table discussing New York Fashion Week is a fantasy. This mindset is saturated in sexism, misogyny, and homophobia. Men who care about fashion are suddenly "gay." Guys who talk about their body dissatisfaction are "sissies."

The real issue is men too terrified to break the barrier.

Dismantling internalized toxic masculinity is the hardest battle I've had to face. It's one that I believe never fades, never can be eradicated from within. I often feel like I'll never be "man enough" for a successful career, a happy relationship, a feeling of inner bliss. And that is directly correlated to the clothing I wear.

Getting dressed is perhaps one of the most difficult everyday obstacles for me—not solely owing to the lack of options, but because of the questions that run wild through my mind: How will this outfit make others perceive me? Is this manly enough? What does this garment combination say about my level of masculinity? While Idris Elba may be able to pull off a hot pink suit on the red carpet, I'm hyperaware—to a fault and personal detriment at times—that my doing so will be viewed as a lack of masculinity, because of my body size and rounded features. High-waisted pants may look perfect on Shawn Mendes. On me, however, they emphasize and showcase my lower stomach, sculpting my body to appear more like that of a curvy woman.

And quite frankly, there's nothing wrong with that. My body shape is naturally how it is, and a stranger's perspective on it is irrelevant to how I should feel. The problem is, however, that for men like me, we sometimes care too much to take that leap into fashion freedom.

"When I started modeling, I saw how you have to look a certain way or be a certain way, either super masculine or super tall," Ady says. "I was even contemplating surgery to lose weight. In the beginning, I would act how I usually don't act just so I can fit in because I wanted to fit. I wanted to become a model in this sector."

Big and tall modeling today often remains reserved for guys who lean more into husky and "built" than fat. Less love handles and more ex-football players, these men are human Adonises with a little more meat packed around the bone. And for those like Ady—who are both visibly queer and higher on the size spectrum—that means feeling welcomed is often out of reach.

The difference is, however, that those like Ady are no longer afraid to hold back. On the contrary, thanks in large part to social media, they can connect over these very failures in the market and speak out for change, much like the many trailblazing women who came before them. Our issues may be vastly different across gender lines, but the blueprint to success remains largely the same.

The fight for size-inclusive menswear has truly just begun. If womenswear itself is still in the introductory phases of change after nearly thirty years of advocacy, then one can only imagine how long the road ahead will be. "It might be a slow climb," Josh says, "and I think we definitely hit some setbacks with COVID for brawn, but the momentum is back." In its half a decade of existence, the big and tall market has pushed to represent one type of man. Now, emboldened and prepared, a full spectrum awaits their place in the limelight.

"I would love to see plus-size menswear editorials from a standpoint that is just so creative and so inspiring and so jaw dropping," says model Thaddeus Coates. "I want that for us and I know it's possible. I want our imaginations to not be tied to the box that has been created for us. I don't want it to just be flannels with chinos and dress shoes."

One of Thaddeus's career highlights came when Rihanna and her team selected him to represent the plus-size menswear expansion of their Savage X Fenty line. It was an indescribable moment for him, one he'll cherish for a lifetime: "[That campaign] spoke to who I am as a personal brand and really leaned into the fact that I'm a Black, queer, plus model."

For Zach—who has celebrated many major wins, from being a guest judge on *America's Next Top Model* to launching his own inclusive swimwear collection labeled Meekos—a top moment came when in 2019 when he became the first brawn model to ever be featured in a luxury brand campaign for his work with Dolce & Gabbana.

"You would never have known [Dolce & Gabbana extended their sizes] because they hadn't announced it yet, but with this campaign featuring Zach, those marketing dollars were put to work to let people know," Josh says, recalling the moment he got the call that the infamous Italian brand wanted to book his top brawn client.

Despite my personal hesitations toward Dolce & Gabbana, witnessing Zach's campaign images go live was a moment that reminded me of the potential within reach. It's easy to feel inferior to the fashion gods of this world when our only options are Old Navy jeans and the occasional Macy's blazer. It's a challenge I encounter every fashion week, every job interview, every Instagram post. How can my exterior match my interior when the options aren't available in such exuberant forms? But as Zach and Thaddeus and Ady and countless other men have proven in those days since 2016, there's room and opportunities for all of us to feel welcomed. It will take work, time, devotion, and upset. But one day it will come true because we are no longer alone. Plus-size men have finally found their community.

For decades, too many of us have lived emotionally secluded from a society that tells us that our existence is a human error. Our minds lead us to believe that our experiences are singular, that we are the only fat ones living in a thin-first world. We shrink our bodies, our personalities, our voices in hopes that we'll be able to hide from the hate that stands beyond our doorways.

But the day we realize we've never been alone is the day we meet ourselves for the first time.

I never knew what it meant to live authentically until I entered the fashion industry. I spent my adolescence playing *other* characters, dictating my thoughts and beliefs on false personas and ideas of what I could become, and never of who I was. That is what the plus-size community has taught me: true self-expression is perhaps the strongest power to exist on this earth. And few will ever get the chance to feel it. I'm one of the fortunate.

Ironically, the power of plus-size fashion has nothing to do with clothing. But it has everything to do with love.

It takes a community to change the world. If the past thirty years have taught us anything, it's that none of this can be done alone. And as we push toward the future, a future of fashion that is all encompassing beyond lines of size, race, and gender, that fact becomes abundantly true.

That future has started to take form within each one of us. Here is what it looks like . . .

11

THE FUTURE OF
FASHION IS FAT

O PRAH WINFREY ONCE SAID, "Surround yourself with only people who are going to lift you higher." For me, that has meant immersing myself within the beauty that is plus-size fashion.

In a world that is so keen on labeling us as "other" just because of the size of our bodies, it is together that we can achieve the previously unimaginable. We often get lost in the negatives, the disappointments; our minds fixate on the challenges that lay before us. But it's impossible to deny how tightly the past three decades have drawn us together—not solely as an industry, as a multibillion-dollar market, as a culture-shifting movement, but as a *community*, one I'm beyond grateful to be a part of.

> I could have never envisioned the adult I am today when I was twelve or thirteen. That version of me wasn't in movies, wasn't in TV, wasn't in magazines, wasn't on the runway. I wouldn't have found her if it wasn't for all the people around me that were also searching for that full version of themselves. Clothes are supposed to serve us, and I would love to see a fashion industry that is really

about serving us, rather than constantly making us feel like we're not enough or are constantly chasing a new goal post.
—**Sean Taylor,** star of Netflix's *The Circle*

I could have never anticipated how monumental my first Chromat runway spectacular would be. In September 2019, eager to make my mark, I begged for a ticket to the brand's tenth-anniversary show at New York Fashion Week. I'd never had the chance to witness Chromat's glory before, but felt an excitement from within that it would be a night to remember.

When I dream of the future of fashion, I envision that Chromat runway. It was bold, authentic, and universally diverse in a manner I'd never seen, not in the pages of *Vogue* or surroundings of my daily life. But one aspect in particular struck a sensitive chord in my heart: plus-size models through the generations brought together for one unifying celebration of love and fashion.

Emme, Hunter McGrady, Denise Bidot, Tess Holliday. It was history, it was present, and it was a revolution, told through their vastly different yet universally relatable stories.

I look back at where I was in high school before I found this community, and it's bleak. Plus-size fashion has legitimately changed my life. I don't know if I would have ever learned to love myself without the community. You may feel lonely, but you are not alone. It's been an absolute honor to go from someone watching this community from the outside to now being able to help inspire others and be a part of all of this.
—**Alex LaRosa-Williams,** model

I made a commitment later that night to dedicate my career to honoring those women, to helping tell their stories in a manner never done before. Because I'd experienced firsthand how life changing their messages of inclusivity are, and more folk from across lines of nation and race and gender and size deserve—rather, *need*—to hear it next.

> Now being older and looking back, I feel like a very proud mom, feeling like I helped steer the ship in plus-size fashion from an early stage. And it really is this proud mom moment where I'm seeing all these brands emerge, seeing all these influencers emerge, and seeing people on the cover of magazines who I never thought I'd see in my lifetime. You have one life to live and you should get out there and enjoy it as much as possible because it's your body. The only thing you should care about is enjoying your life.
> —**Nicole Phillips,** marketing and communications professional

Plus-size fashion has always been and will always be about infinitely more than clothing. It is about unity, empowerment, and transformation. It is about stepping into your power, letting your soul shine through. It is about finally feeling confident in the very skin this society has tried—and failed—to rip to shreds. It is my firmest belief that the future of fashion is *all of us*. We are what will propel it, what will fuel its core. It will not only welcome us all into the conversation but also elevate and prioritize our voices in the very way we've longed to see.

But there's more work to do before we can get there.

> Inclusive fashion is a team sport—there are so many different groups and individuals that have to work together to create the ecosystem that we aspire to create. This team sport is successful because at the core of this incredibly

diverse community are some very, very strong shared experiences. All said and done, when I reflect on the last several years, I am left with the strong conviction that the future of fashion is bright. It's a future where the power of fashion and freedom of style is available to everybody. After all, the more we're able to express ourselves the more we learn about ourselves and others, and that's one of the most powerful things that we can be a part of.

—**Nadia Boujarwah,** founder of Dia & Co

What's next is perhaps what's hardest: we must first heal and reconcile from within the community itself. For too long, we've allowed racism to thrive within our inclusive subset of the market. That is what must change *now*. There is no room here for hatred or anti-Blackness; there is no room for Asian or Latinx hate and discrimination. The longer we allow these issues to fester, the more difficult it will be to make plus-size fashion the norm.

We must use our voices to advocate for a full spectrum of representation. That includes those of higher sizes beyond a 3X. No brand can ever accomplish "fashion for every woman" when their very size range is exclusive of millions.

I long for the day when fashion is truly inclusive of *all*. I can't wait for the day a size 6 and a size 30 have access to the same kind of clothes across different price points and aesthetics. The plus-size fashion community has been an integral part of my self-love journey. Since college, plus-size influencers like Gabi Gregg, Nicolette Mason, Kellie Brown, and others have been positive role models who have shown me it's more than possible to live a full, well-rounded life as a plus person despite what society at large may say. Seeing them have fun with fashion in ways I thought unimaginable gave me the confidence to go outside of my comfort zone and wear silhouettes and bold colors as a Black plus-size woman. We need to continue to pour love into ourselves and try our best to drown out any negativity, especially on those down days. Your body is an amazing vehicle that has gotten you through so much in life. Honor and cherish it.

—**Shammara Lawrence,** cofounder of the Power of Plus digital platform

No brand is perfect. No singular person can flawlessly enact change. That makes it all the more important to represent a full range of perspectives and voices behind the scenes. We are each the storytellers of our own journeys, and there is room for all of us at the table.

It's hard to put into words how much being a part of the plus-size fashion community has changed my life. When I first discovered this community, I didn't believe that I was worthy of being seen, and I felt like no one cared about what I had to say. I've learned that there's so much value in our stories because when we exist outside of the norm, being in front of the camera shows that we deserve to take up space. And I would not have gotten to that point, personally without the many, many women who came before me. I want everyone to have access to style and the things that make them feel good. Even with all of the progress that we've made over the past five years, so many people are still left out of this conversation, so we really need to widen who has access to be able to wear what they want and dress how they want.

—**Alysse Dalessandro,** influencer and blogger of *Ready to Stare*

To be a changemaker requires stepping outside one's comfort zone to bridge the gaps that divide communities. The grandest take-away of being the "other" is we know how powerful it is to finally feel as though your voice and your presence matter enough to be recognized. The truth is that not every plus-size woman, man, and person knows that yet. And that is why we must continue to push.

> Joining this community has been like stepping inside of this beautiful bubble that I didn't know existed. The acceptance, encouragement, confidence, and relatability of being surrounded by people going through life as a plus-size person was completely life changing. Just as people follow me and tell me that through sharing my experience or dressing my body at my size might help them, I want future generations to feel the same way. I want them to appreciate their body as it is and feel that freedom to dress how they want, not feeling like they have to cover up. I want them to reach a level of freedom coming out of the gates that we never had.
> —**Erica Lauren,** model

It sometimes becomes easy to feel tokenized, to feel as though you're the only one fighting the good fight. And while the fashion industry at large may try and pin us up against each other, it's vital to our success—of both our movement and community—that we break through that noise and stigma to remind ourselves why all this work matters.

> The opposite of inclusivity is truly divisiveness, and I feel like we've always felt othered and different and not good enough, and only recently have companies started to cater to us. I think the future of fashion is when this doesn't

have to be a conversation anymore because it's already normalized. Plus-size fashion has allowed me to come alive with a person, and to really fully express who I am. What makes you unique, what makes you think you're just so different from other people, what makes you stand out and not fit in is exactly what the world needs and exactly what you were created for.

—**Alex Michael May,** influencer

Think of how far we've come together: A new wave of super-models who reflect what we actually look like has emerged. Retail brands have expanded their sizes to the point where we don't have to worry about acquiring last-minute date night or job interview ensembles. Social media is filled with individuals across the globe sharing their personal, touching stories about self-acceptance and body love. And as those conversations intensify and spread, they become all the more common.

More than anything—more than clothes themself or any style—I think the future is going to be a lot more plus-size bodies wearing whatever the hell they want, feeling empowered to be seen, instead of spending our lives covered up. The future is a lot more bold than what we've lived so far. All I've ever wanted to do is impart how I feel to others and give them the power to not be afraid. If the mom in the middle of Iowa finally puts on a bikini for the first time in her life when she takes her kids to the lake, then all of my work is worth it. Remember that you don't have to dull out your shine for the people who don't want you to shine as bright.

—**Natalie Hage,** influencer

Soon, the days of waiting outside the Zara dressing rooms for your thin friends to finish trying on their medium-sized clothes will be over. We won't have to sweat it, because brands that care and prioritize our needs will continue to lead the way.

> When people walk through the doors of the Plus Bus, they are often transported, transformed, and really moved, because so many people have had traumatic shopping memories. So when you come into a space like the Plus Bus where you can touch and feel all of the brands in person and it's a space just for you, it's pretty magical, and we need more of that. Even though my wallet may not like it, the idea that I can have access to Versace and to Badgley Mischka and Michael Kors is really exciting, and I think that will only continue to grow in the future.
>
> —**Marcy Guevara-Prete,** co-owner of the Plus Bus Boutique

Soon we'll be able to breathe, and how amazing will that finally feel?

> I've been a big girl my whole life and struggled to find things to wear as a result. My life got smaller and smaller. I didn't go out, I didn't go to parties or events because I didn't have anything to wear. That created a sense of shame. I hear a lot about how plus-size women lack confidence, but the reality is what we lack is clothing to wear. In our twenty years, I am beyond proud that we set out to serve the consumer who has been underserved and continue to do so everyday. We've made it our mission to be their one-stop shop, provide expert-fitting clothing, while also creating a platform that inspires them to be unstoppable.
>
> —**Liz Muñoz,** CEO of Torrid

For the young girls who begin dieting as early as elementary school; for the boys who feel they're too fat to ever be loved; for the teens who begin to starve themselves, who purge and conceal and hurt so deeply; for the moms who refuse to ever go to the beach; for the women who hide and cover up and question why they've been burdened with the curse of fatness: You are not alone. Not now, not tomorrow, not ever. Because we've fought for this community to withstand rejection, exile, silencing, even a global pandemic. And we're not going anywhere.

The future of fashion can feel like a supreme fantasy. And perhaps that's where all realities start. Because as we push further and further, as we fight for size inclusivity to penetrate the deepest sections of this industry and society, we see that fantasy begin to take shape. We each have our individual dreams of what exactly that day will look like, but we feel a universal longing for the day when all of this is so normal that it's no longer a conversation that needs to be had; the day when the term *plus size* will be thrown away; the day when we'll take up as much space as our fat little butts deserve.

This is the future we're fighting for. *We* are the future.

ACKNOWLEDGMENTS

THE POWER OF PLUS exists because of the community behind it—a community that gave me purpose, that blazed a trail for my voice to even exist, and that saved my life.

First and foremost, thank you to my agent, JL Stermer of Next Level Lit, for recognizing my passion, trusting my vision, and for bringing it all to life in a way I could have never imagined. I grow more grateful everyday for our fateful meeting and can't wait to keep changing the world together.

To Kara Rota, my editor at Chicago Review Press: I always knew it would be *you*. From our first phone call, before an idea or manuscript or proposal was written, I knew it would be *you*. Thank you for giving *The Power of Plus* a platform and for caring so deeply about true, authentic, impactful inclusivity. I have nothing but gratitude for the rest of the CRP team: Allison Felus, Frances Giguette, Devon Freeny, Hailey Peterson, Melanie Roth, Chelsea Balesh, Anisha Wilson, Natalya Balnova, et al.

To Shammara Lawrence, my incredible business partner and confidant, with whom our beautiful digital community around this book came to life: I will forever believe we were destined to meet. And I'm so grateful we did.

Behind every book is a family prepared to preorder and hype an author up at a moment's notice. Mine is rather eclectic.

To my parents, Anna and Giuseppe, who fought and worked to give us a better life in a foreign country; to Vincenzo, for accompanying me on my many New York City excursions on the hunt for purpose in this magnificent city; to Alex, for acceptance; to Amber, for the Friendly's ice cream trips, and for being my sister; and to Briana, for the loudest car ride singalongs.

To Zio Sergio, for showing me that potential and dreams are simply reality waiting to be pursued; to Zia Stephany, for teaching me to be brave and bold in ways I'm still grasping; to Zio Stefano, for showing me what family truly means; and to Zio Sal and Zia Sue, for taking me to my first Broadway show, igniting a flame in my heart that will never be extinguished.

To my cousins, whom I refuse to rank in order of favorites, despite the ever-growing pressure to do so. I love each one of you deeply. To Aiko, and to my rather large family in Italy, the fellow Russos and beyond: my love for you is like the courses at a Sunday dinner—never-ending.

To Alma Esposito, for bringing us all together. And Ciro Esposito, who lived to see us succeed.

In loving memory of Gabriella Russo and Nicholas Esposito. We think of you both, forever and always.

NOTES

1. Building the Mold

The Venus of Willendorf: Joshua Learn, "What Did the Venus of Willendorf Originally Represent?," *Discover*, March 5, 2021.

Among one of the first: "Lena Bryant Malsin," Jewish Virtual Library, accessed November 21, 2021, https://www.jewishvirtuallibrary.org /lena-bryant-malsin.

bust, waist, and hip measurements: Ginia Bellafante, "Plus-Size Wars," *New York Times*, July 28, 2010.

This fatphobic stigma: Lauren Downing Peters, "Flattering the Figure, Fitting In: The Design Discourses of Stoutwear, 1915–1930," *Fashion Theory*, 23:2, 167–194, https://doi.org/10.1080/1362704X.2019.1567059.

fraudulent "obesity epidemic": Your Fat Friend, "The Bizarre and Racist History of the BMI," Elemental by Medium, October 15, 2019, https://elemental .medium.com/the-bizarre-and-racist-history-of-the-bmi-7d8dc2aa33bb.

the National Bureau of Standards: Laura Stampler, "The Bizarre History of Women's Clothing Sizes," *Time*, October 23, 2014, https://time .com/3532014/women-clothing-sizes-history/.

Taking to the streets: Dan Fletcher, "The Fat Acceptance Movement," *Time*, July 31, 2009, http://content.time.com/time/nation/article /0,8599,1913858,00.html.

In February 1978: Gay Pauley, "Mary Duffy Runs Model Agency a Premise 'Big Is Beautiful,'" United Press International, January 24, 1984, https:// www.upi.com/Archives/1984/01/24/Mary-Duffy-runs-model-agency-a -premise-big-is-beautiful/4727443768400/.

According to a 1984 United Press: Pauley, "Mary Duffy."

change was constant: Rob Stafford Hagwood, "Couture Plus Clothes for Large-Sized Women Now Are a Big Part of Top Designers' Collections," *Sun Sentinel*, June 9, 1991, https://www.sun-sentinel.com/news/fl-xpm -1991-06-09-9103020860-story.html

2. The Digital Touch

Toccara Jones made history: *America's Next Top Model*, season 3, episode 1, "The Girl with the Secret," aired September 22, 2004, on UPN, https:// www.hulu.com/series/americas-next-top-model.

The first time I experienced this: Gianluca Russo, "In Its Fifth Year, CurvyCon Proves the Future of Fashion Is Fat," Fashionista.com, September 11, 2019, https://fashionista.com/2019/09/the-curvy-con-2019-plus-size -fashion.

3. The New Supers

with the backing of IMG's reputation: Lauren Chan, "IMG Signs Five Plus-Size Models," *Vogue Italia*, January 31, 2015, https://www.vogue.it/en /vogue-curvy/curvy-news/2014/01/img-signs-plus-size-models-; brackets in original.

The debate around the term: Gianluca Russo, "Is It Time to Retire the Term *Plus-Size*?," Glamour.com, August 27, 2019, https://www.glamour.com /story/term-plus-sized-debate.

A pivotal moment: Gianluca Russo, "Claiming Space: 26 People Talk Being Fat and Working in Fashion," Nylon.com, September 9, 2019, https:// www.nylon.com/being-fat-working-in-fashion.

5. The Body Boom

68 percent of American women: Hilary George-Parkin, "Size, by the Numbers," Racked.com, June 5, 2018, https://www.racked.com/2018/6/5/17380662 /size-numbers-average-woman-plus-market.

"For so long, I loved you": Chastity Garner Valentine, "#BoycottingTarget #Altuzarra-ForTarget," *Garnerstyle*, August 15, 2014, https://www.garnerstyle.com /2014/08/im-boycotting-target-altuzarra-for-target.html.

6. Runways and Redemption

According to the Fashion Spot's: Heather Cichowski, "Report: Racial, Size and Age Diversity Inch Forward, Gender Inclusivity Drops for Fashion Month Spring 2020," The Fashion Spot, October 16, 2019, https://www.thefashionspot.com/runway-news/847460-diversity-report-fashion-month-spring-2020/.

That number dwindled: Morgan C. Schimminger, "Report: Racial Diversity Ticks Up Slightly, Size, Age and Gender Representation All Drop for Fashion Month Spring 2021," The Fashion Spot, October 19, 2020, https://www.thefashionspot.com/runway-news/858789-diversity-report-fashion-month-spring-2021/.

A report from InStyle: Tess Garcia, "More Fashion Week Designers Are Making Plus-Size Clothing, but There's a Catch," *InStyle*, February 14, 2020, https://www.instyle.com/fashion/runway/fashion-week-size-report-fall-2020.

7. Rewriting the Fantasy

In an interview with Vogue: Nicole Phelps, "The Architects of the Victoria's Secret Fashion Show Are Still Banking on Bombshells," *Vogue*, November 8, 2018, https://www.vogue.com/article/victorias-secret-ed-razek-monica-mitro-interview.

giving me the exclusive: Gianluca Russo, "ThirdLove Responds to Victoria's Secret Exec Ed Razek's Comments About Their Brands," Teenvogue.com, November 19, 2018, https://www.teenvogue.com/story/thirdlove-response-victorias-secret-ed-razek-interview.

8. Let Us Vogue

the publication's website rose 200 percent: Ruby Warrington, "Inside Teen Vogue: 'Our Readers Consider Themselves Activists,'" *Guardian*, February 25, 2017, https://www.theguardian.com/media/2017/feb/25/teen-vogue-readers-consider-themselves-activists.

I emailed my editor with a pitch: Gianluca Russo, "Dolce and Gabbana's 'Chinese Chopsticks' Ad Isn't the Only Reason We Should Stop Supporting Them," teenvogue.com, November 21, 2018, https://www.teenvogue

.com/story/dolce-gabbana-chinese-chopsticks-ad-isnt-the-only-reason -we-should-stop-supporting-them.

9. The Racial Divide

As explained in depth: Sabrina Strings, *Fearing the Black Body: The Racial Origins of Fat Phobia* (New York University Press, 2019).

10. The Brawn Boys

This, however, is different: Mary Nell Trautner, Samantha Kwan, and Scott V. Savage, "Masculinity, Competence, and Health: The Influence of Weight and Race on Social Perceptions of Men," *Men and Masculinities* 16, no. 4 (October 2013): 432–51, https://doi.org/10.1177/1097184X13502667.

INDEX